The Artist & The Quilt

The Artist & The Quilt

EDITED BY CHARLOTTE ROBINSON

Alfred A. Knopf
New York

To past generations of our mothers, who
have kept the art of quilt making alive.

To my mother, Charlotte Moore Hill, whose legacy of
fine needlework was an inspiration for this project.

And to my daughters, Liz, Mary Lynn, and Sally.

ACKNOWLEDGMENTS

This book was a delight to compile, for it gives me reason, once again, to thank the generous and gifted people who came together to celebrate one of the truly indigenous art forms in America, the quilt.

I wish to acknowledge a special debt to the women who were the designers and makers of the twenty quilts that form the core of this collaboration. In particular, I would like to mention Marcia King, who frequently and generously offered her New York loft to exhibit the quilts to critics, museum staff, and collectors. Special thanks also to Miriam Schapiro, who shared her deep well of knowledge, her endless list of friends, and her essay. And, special thanks to Joyce Kozloff, Ellen Lanyon, Mary Beth Edelson, and Betye Saar, who did their utmost to ensure an audience for our project. Isabel Bishop and Faith Ringgold lent a special kind of moral support. Marilyn Lanfear, Maggie Saunders, Glenna Park, Betty Ward Johnson, and John Leeper in San Antonio, Texas, at the Marion Koogler McNay Art Institute, who went to extraordinary lengths to insure a gala opening for the exhibition's tour.

My husband, Robby, and other members of my family patiently helped and coped with piles of papers, finished and unfinished quilts, and endless cold dinners. They are: Robin, Larry, Ron, Tobie, Ellie, Elizabeth, Torrance, and Luke.

David Tannous never failed in his efforts to give me cool-headed advice, and an occasional push, whenever I faltered. Lyndia Terr, Kate Roberts, and Honey Nashman spent much of their time on this project and, along with Joan Mister and Ruth Corning, guided me over rough roads with cheerful words. Penny McMorris and Paul Lopez produced a splendid film of our project, and Larry Singer generously gave endless legal advice. All of the contributors to this book have provided inspiration.

I would like to express appreciation to Michael Friedman at Quarto for believing in this book. Special thanks to the editors at Quarto and Knopf, Marta Hallett and Susan Ralston, for their skill and patience, and to Sophie Burnham, who edited my introduction and helped me to keep a fresh perspective.

Others who helped: Sally and David Alne, Sandy Augliere, Kitty Bahnsen, Lena Behme, Norma Broude, Alice Clagett, Minna Cook, Roberta Emerson, Francis Farr, Lillie Fetter, Mary Graves, Betty Guy, Ann Harris, Nancy Heflin, Harriet Lyons, Mitzi Landau, Mary Lanier, Helen Messinger, Cynthia Nadelman, Sue Pierce, Cynthia Redick, Barbara Rigdon, Dorothy Seiberling, Charlotte Sheedy, Gena Simpson, Ann Van DeVanter, Nancy Wallace, Kathy Williams, and Austin Wood.

To colleagues at Rutgers University: Evelyn Apgar, Coordinator of the Women Artists Series at Douglas College and Phillip Dennis Cate, Director, Jane Voorhees Zimmerli Museum at Rutgers University, many thanks.

I have not the space nor has the reader the patience for the many other people who helped, but they know who they are. I am deeply grateful for their help.

Charlotte Robinson

THIS IS A BORZOI BOOK

Published by Alfred A. Knopf, Inc.

Copyright © 1983 by Quarto Marketing Ltd.

Published in the United States by Alfred A. Knopf, Inc., New York
Distributed by Random House, Inc., New York

Library of Congress Catalog Card Number: 83-47775

Library of Congress Cataloging in Publication Data
Main entry under title:

The Artist & the quilt

Catalog of a collection of quilts exhibited in museums in San Antonio,
Sept. 10–Oct. 22, 1983, and other cities.
Includes bibliographies and index.
1. Quilts—United States—History—20th century—Exhibitions.
2.Women artists—United States—Exhibitions.
I. Robinson, Charlotte, 1924–   . II. Title:
Artist and the quilt.
NK9112.A74 1983   746.9′7′0973074013   83-47775
ISBN 0-394-53220-1
ISBN 0-394-71560-8 (pbk.)

THE ARTIST & THE QUILT
was prepared and produced by Quarto Marketing Ltd.
32–33 Kingly Court, London W. 1, England

Editor: Marta Hallett
Art Director/Designer: Richard Boddy

Typeset by BPE Graphics, Inc.

Color Separations by Hong Kong Scanner Craft Company Ltd.

Printed and bound in Hong Kong by Leefung-Asco Printers Ltd.

C O N T E N T S

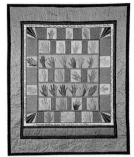

SIGNATURE QUILT NO. 1
Designed and cut by
Charlotte Robinson
with assistance from
Daphne Shuttleworth
and
Ruth Corning.
Silk-screened by
Wenda F. von Weise.
Pieced by
Bonnie Persinger
with assistance from
Betty Guy,
Gina Simpson, Honey Nashman,
and
Lena Behme.
Hand-embroidered by
Alice Clagett,
Barbara Rigdon,
Cynthia Redick,
Sandy Augliere
and
ten members of the
Quilt Research Staff.
Hand-quilted by
Bob Douglas
1982
Raw Silk and Cotton
96″x 79″

THE MITCHELL FAMILY QUILT
Rosemary Wright,
&
The Mitchell Family,
Quilted by
Bob Douglas
1983
Cotton
88″x 84″

THE ROAD TO THE
CENTER OF THE WORLD
Alice Baber
&
Edith Mitchell
1980
Cotton and Silk
92″x 48″

STARWORT PHENOMENA
Ellen Lanyon
&
Angela Jacobi
1981
Cotton and Silk
93″x 69″

MRS. OLIVER BYRNE'S QUILT
Elaine Lustig Cohen
&
Sharon McKain
Pieced by
Sharon McKain,
Quilted by
Rosalia Mehringer
1981
Cotton
70″x 85″

PATANG
Lynda Benglis
&
Amy Chamberlin
1980
Cotton/Satin/Silk
94″x 75″

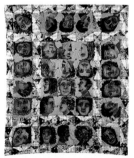

ECHOES OF HARLEM
Faith Ringgold
&
Willi Posey
1980
Hand-painted Cotton
100″x 96″

FANTASIES
Betye Saar
&
Judy Mathieson
1981
Cotton
86″x 61″

UNTITLED
Dorothy Gillespie
&
Bonnie Persinger
1982
Cotton
108″x 45″

WOMEN RISING
Mary Beth Edelson
&
Marie Griffin Ingalls
1977
Cotton
85"x85"

FAN LADY MEETS
RUFFLED WATERS
Harmony Hammond
&
Bob Douglas
1983
Cotton
75"x90"

THE BLUE NILE
Charlotte Robinson
&
Bonnie Persinger
1982
Cotton and Silk
104"x77"

UNTITLED
Betty Parsons
&
Amy Chamberlin
1980
Cotton/Velveteen/Corduroy
71"x96"

CANTILEVER
**Marcia King,
Bob Douglas**
&
Nancy Vogel
1982
Cotton
72"x103"

OLIVIA IN BLUE HAT
Alice Neel
&
Chris Wolf Edmonds
1981
Cotton
75"x43"

UNTITLED
Joyce Kozloff
&
Patricia Newkirk
1981
Cotton
101"x73"

A QUILT IS A COVER
Marilyn Lanfear
&
Theresa Helms
1981
Cotton and Silk
80"x87"

VARIATIONS ON THE
THEME OF WALKING, II
Isabel Bishop
&
Wenda F. von Weise
1981
Raw Silk and Cotton
76"x65"

THE PHOENIX HEART
Miriam Schapiro
&
Marilyn Price,
Assisted by
**Carol Clemons,
Virginia Koehler,
Mary Kay Horn,
Beryl Poland,**
and
Janet Robertson
1981
Hand Silk-screened
Cotton
82"x82"

SIGNATURE QUILT No. 2
Quilt Research Staff
1983
Raw Silk and Cotton
114"x90"

THE QUILT PROJECT
A Personal Memoir

In the heady atmosphere of the 1970s, amidst the excitement of the Women's Movement, three artists from New York and Washington, D.C., Dorothy Gillespie, Alice Baber, and I, were discussing the ways in which women were bringing their own experiences —their personal female vision—into mainstream art through such unusual media as performance, body art, diaries, weaving, and even china painting and needlework. We conceived the idea of celebrating the year 1975—designated by the United Nations as the "International Year of the Woman"—by asking prominent women artists to design

Seated, front (left to right): *Barbara Rigdon, Sarah Tuft, Marcia King, Alice Clagett, Rosemary Wright, Helen Messenger, Daphne Shuttleworth, Charlotte Robinson, Sally Alne, Kate Roberts, Claudia Vess, Sandy Augliere, Sydney Lowenthal (with baby);* Standing, back (left to right): *Alice Simms, Bonnie Persinger, Ruth Corning, Bob Douglas, Joan Mister, Honey Nashman, Amy Chamberlin, Mary Graves, Lillie Fetter, Lena Behme.*

two hundred years ago by women who, with no formal education, mastered the exacting geometry of complex, hard-edged quilting. White-on-white was a prototype for minimal art, while appliqué and trapunto were stitched like bas relief sculpted into stone.

By focusing on the quilt as an art form, we would be making a statement about our identities as artists, as female artists governed by both masculine and feminine principles, and shaped by our cultural conditioning. We would explore a rich history that runs from the padded clothing of ancient Persia to the highly

quilts. There was a certain irony to our idea. Nothing has been more crucial to the radical changes in the art of this century than the eagerness of artists to experiment with new media, especially those using high technology, in order to expand the definition of what art comprises. Yet "new" in this case meant a form of art practiced by women for four hundred years and, for the most part, reserved exclusively for them. We were considering a return to a truly indigenous art form in order to celebrate a contemporary phenomenon: the Women's Movement.

From the beginning we were anxious to eliminate the hierarchical division between fine arts and crafts that has evolved over the last three hundred years, that separation between visually distinguished articles created for aesthetic pleasure and those created for practical use. Quilts, defined as articles made for practical use, have been excluded from consideration as fine or mainstream art. Yet there is nothing "unartistic" about the medium. Op art, a favored genre of the 1960s, was foreshadowed

developed quilts of eighteenth-century England, and to American Colonial patchworks born of the absence of fabrics and made one square at a time under the harshest pioneer conditions. We were acknowledging the chain connecting contemporary women with generations of their mothers—a fusion of past and present and a recognition that we, as contemporary women artists, form a part of that continuum.

Looking back seven years to that conversation, we appear so innocent! Had we known the obstacles or guessed the difficulties we would face, I doubt that we would have taken the first step toward executing our idea. We were blessed with ignorance.

Whatever you can do or dream you can, begin it;
Boldness has genius, power and magic in it. —Goethe

What plans we made! An exhibition of twenty quilts, sewn by the finest needleworkers and shown with the original artwork of mature, established women artists, would be circulated to art museums around the country, with the hope that the effort would enrich the experience of other artists and push back the frontiers of our perceptions.

Only occasionally in the past decade have quilts been shown in art museums as examples of fine art. I make a distinction here between showing quilts and showing them *as art*, for of course they have been shown in textile museums, in historic houses, and at the Smithsonian Institution, as examples of Colonial history and technology. In 1971 Jonathan Holstein broke through the barrier when he organized the exhibition "Abstract Designs in American Quilts" at the Whitney Museum in New York. Most recently, the stunning "Baltimore Album Quilts" opened at the Museum of Fine Arts in Houston, traveled to the Metropolitan Museum in New York, and closed at the Baltimore Museum. These exhibits broke attendance records and ensured a place in art history for antique quilts. Why do so many people prefer the antique over the contemporary? Is it because the quality is higher, the variety greater? Or simply because we revere the old?

How to begin? Our first need was for a finished quilt, a prototype to show to others invited to participate. But before you make a quilt, you need a quilter. For months we searched the Washington-area quilt exhibitions. After half a year we spotted a design so fresh and original, sewn with such impeccable skill, that we knew we had found our first needle artist. The piece looked like an ear of corn, a soft sculpture made to stand proudly in a collector's living room. Closer examination revealed a puffy yellow quilt rolled up and tucked into a stitched green fabric husk, ready at a moment's notice to be "husked" and used as a bedcover. The person with the artistry and imagination to create this quilt was Bonnie Persinger. We soon enticed her into the project to make the first quilt, from my design.

Like paintings, quilts offer great freedom of choice in color, form, and texture. Our goal was to explore new imagery and techniques. I wanted to use the image of a river (part of a series on which I was currently working), but this design, with its curved lines and soft edges, its melting, blending colors, was difficult to translate into fabric. Bonnie fearlessly plunged in, inventing a form of machine embroidery. Using her needle much as an artist uses a brush, she covered the sharp edges of the fabric with sparkling layers of thread, creating an illusion of colors running together in an easy flow.

With this prototype in hand, we hoped to interest other artists in the project. But immediately we faced the question of money.

"The lilies of the field may need no raiment," said my friend Sophie Burnham, "but they are fertilized by the hand of man." Our most constant problem was funding. The need for it began immediately and never seemed to end, creating painful episodes, disrupting relationships. Much of the early money came from my own pocket, and from the beginning it loomed as a monstrous outlay. Everyone knows of artists' need for money; that of the quilters is equally large. It is important to note that in the end the quilters, the needle artists who executed the designs, were paid only two hundred fifty dollars each, through grants, for work that took them weeks and months of concentrated effort. The artists received no compensation for their designs.

But in the beginning, ignorant as lilies in our innocence, we did not comprehend the depths of the problem of money. One day we met a man who volunteered to raise the necessary money for our project. We were overjoyed! A fundraiser seemed too good to be true.

We arranged a meeting at Dorothy Gillespie's New York studio with this gentleman, six of the artists, and two quilters. Bonnie Persinger showed our prototype quilt and her friend Amy Chamberlin (who was later to work on the beautiful designs of Lynda Benglis and Betty Parsons) showed examples of her machine-quilting techniques. Mary Beth Edelson was there, and Joyce Kozloff, Alice Neel, and Miriam Schapiro. They appreciated our idea. They wanted to work on designs. Then came the spectre of money. The more our "fundraiser" talked, describing the great sum he would raise and where it would go, the more the artists quite rightly questioned how much would go to them. They wanted a written legal contract before turning over their designs—on this the project threatened to founder.

Bonnie, Amy, and I returned to Washington. Our financial wizard resigned. We learned later he was interested in our nameless project only because he thought his girlfriend might make a quilt; when she left him, he left us. I hung my quilt in my studio and went back to my paintings.

It was 1976. The International Year of the Woman was over.

In 1977 the quilt was still hanging on my wall when Jim Melchert, then Director of Visual Arts for the National Endowment for the Arts, stopped by. We talked of the aborted project. He liked this "marriage of fine art and folk art," as he called it, and encouraged me to apply to the NEA for a grant. One of the exponential effects of writing a grant proposal is that it forces you to answer serious questions: Why is this project important? Who will benefit? What will it cost? In the struggle to fill out the necessary forms you begin to articulate the ideas swimming like elvers in your head.

Months later the NEA granted us three thousand dollars, a sum just large enough to pay twelve quilters a small honorarium each for making one quilt. The Endowment grant also provided emotional encouragement and the stamp of official approval that could attract other support. By then it was 1978. Little did we know that it would take years to complete the quilts.

Meanwhile, through my good friend Dr. Susan Dees of Durham, North Carolina, I was fortunate enough to meet Mary Duke Biddle Semans, president of the Mary Duke Biddle Foundation. Mary has a deep respect for the art of quilting. She instantly grasped the concept and through her foundation provided a grant to underwrite documentation, which was to be administered by the North Carolina Museum of Art in Raleigh. Moussa Domit, the Director, agreed to have the museum sponsor the exhibition, publish a catalogue, and administer the exhibition both during its formation and when it traveled to other institutions. In addition, he provided several thousand invaluable dollars to help cover administrative costs. Especially in the beginning, when we were struggling to grow, this commitment was priceless, although the exhibition and catalogue failed to materialize under the auspices of the museum. After Mr. Domit left the North Carolina Museum in 1980, Gay Hertzman, Acting Director, and Lorraine Lasslet, Director of Affiliate Galleries, administered the Semans Grant for "The Artist and the Quilt," but by then, being better organized, we were able to stand on our own.

Throughout this period, over months that grew to years, we continued to hone our objectives. There was the question, for example, of materials. In the summer of 1978 I had seen a quilt in Chicago that fascinated me. Artist Margaret Wharton had made it, cutting up beer cans, flattening them, sewing them

Bonnie Boudra Persinger with her inspirational corn quilt.

with wire, and mounting them on black velvet as a "crazy quilt." She hung the work at the foot of her stairs, where, seen from above, it shone like satin. This started a new line of thinking: Should we make quilts out of metal or wood or paper, or in odd sizes? To find answers I traveled to six Texas museums, asking directors and curators how they would put together a quilt show.

Effie Rae Bateman and quilter Marie Griffin Ingalls proudly display the Edelson/Ingalls quilt.

Quilting bee in Charlotte Robinson's studio doubles as a corporate board meeting for members of the Quilt Research Staff. From left: Bob Douglas, Lillie Fetter, Mary Graves, Sally Alne, Lena Behme, and Bonnie Persinger.

How many quilts? What materials should we use? What should we name our project? I received different answers from each of the eight people I interviewed. Don Goodal, Director of Galleries for the University of Texas, gave advice that stuck with me: "Make up your mind about what you want to say with the exhibition, state the facts in the open, cover yourself with a forthright history of the project, then stand back for the flak."

There have been times when the flak has almost buried the project.

Janet Mack, then Curator at the McNay Art Institute in San Antonio, was another of those interviewed. It was she who came up with our title, and she who suggested that making quilts of unusual materials would present problems for the exhibiting museums. "The connotation of the word 'quilt' is bedcover. Better stick to fabrics," she said.

I developed a love-hate relationship with quilts. Despite my determination to do the exhibition, it took time from my own work (what is more precious to an artist?), and it took money. It became all-consuming. Our 1970s ideal of a participatory democracy, a fluid structure of command, gave way to the practical exigencies of a single administrator, one person determined to see the project through.

With guidelines in place, with seed money for the quilters, with support from a foundation, the next step was to find the needlewomen. I made several trips to North Carolina, partly to satisfy the Biddle Foundation's requirement that its grants benefit the people of North Carolina or of New York.

The results were not always encouraging. On the first trip I approached a traditional quilter about making a quilt for us. She explained that she had just sold a work to Walter Cronkite for five hundred dollars: "Me and my daughter can sit in front of the TV, turning out four or five patchworks in a winter without hardly looking down. If I took one of your quilts I'd have to concentrate on it all year."

Then we came across Effie Rae Bateman, owner and operator of an extraordinary art gallery, Eiis (pronounced *Ee-eyes*) Little Corner of the World. It is in Belle Haven, North Carolina, just a stone's throw from the inland waterway. This remarkable woman had transformed an old filling station, her inheritance from her husband, into an art gallery. The grease trough became a reflecting pool; a collection of old windshields became elegant transparent shelves. By building on different interior elevations, she created an illusion of a vast open space, in which all sorts of arts and crafts were displayed. Effie Rae's energy and magic touch offer area artists an opportunity to show their work to the many "collectors" whose boats ply the nearby waterway.

It was Effie Rae who rounded up quilters from the area and served cold cider in a handmade pottery bowl while Bonnie Persinger, Dorothy Gillespie, and I looked at their needlework. We explained our project. We invited one of them, Marie Ingalls, to join our effort, and she agreed to work on the quilt of Mary Beth Edelson.

And so quilters, one by one, were enlisted. But equally exciting was another effect of our visit. A year later, at Effie Rae's invitation, the three of us traveled back to Belle Haven to act as jury for a quilt show sponsored by Eiis Little Corner of the World. We found that many of the quilters, inspired by our project, had submitted quilts of original and untraditional designs! Were we already helping, then, to built the network of artists that we had originally imagined in those talks so many years earlier? And nothing in a museum yet!

Now we are finished with our project. Seven years have passed. Eighteen graphic artists have given designs to sixteen needle artists, who have executed quilts of exquisite proportions and differing aims.

Many others have also worked on this project. Thirty-five women worked as volunteers to sew the two signature quilts seen on the front and back covers of this book. There were seventeen embroiderers, none of them paid a penny; ten women who made themselves available to take my calls at any hour; one who kept a running record of the changing addresses, phone numbers, marital status, babies, and general news of the more than fifty women who participated in the project. Some women worked on publicity and others on resumés—no mean task when you consider that the resumé of Betty Parsons alone runs twenty-five pages. How could we reduce it to one page and still show the dimensions of her artistic career?

Some of these volunteers, the needle artists, have told me what they derived from the experience—a community of spirit in the gentle rhythm of their needlework, the trading of stories, the heightening of consciousness, touching at the very roots of their being; for sewing is a quieting, steadying enterprise, like stroking an animal.

Respectful recognition is due these volunteers. The project could not have succeeded without all of us working together. Some, but not all, of the volunteers have seen their names sewn into the signature quilts. I hope the reader will pause a moment to read their names on the acknowledgments page, consider their contribution, and reflect on the words of one volunteer, Lyndia Terr, a member of our research staff: "The project doesn't emphasize one woman's imagery. I have seen so many different points of view expressed that it reinforces my conviction that my own viewpoint is valid. The experience of working with these established artists has expanded my imagery and given validity to my work. It also taught me that nothing is really finished."

I hope that is so. I hope our work will act as a seed that will flower later, and reseed, and grow again, unfinished for many years to come.   CHARLOTTE ROBINSON/1982

Daphne Shuttleworth and Ruth Corning working on designs for Signature *quilts in the Robinson studio in 1981.*

Attending the quilt preview in Marcia King's New York loft: Annie Shaver Crandall and Eleanor Munro (above left); Max Kozloff and Ellen Lanyon (above right); and Dorothy Seiberling (bottom right), in September, 1981.

Miriam Schapiro, Alice Neel, and Betty Parsons preparing for the PBS filming at Robinson's studio.

CHAPTER 1

AMERICAN QUILTS: 1770-1880

JEAN TAYLOR FEDERICO

Although quilting was an integral part of the lives of many women, very little is known about the individuals who quilted in eighteenth- and nineteenth-century America. Because few women wrote about their daily lives, today one tends to recreate, define, and understand the past from the objects on hand. Often this study has been colored by a large measure of folk tradition provided by the late-nineteenth-century romancers of the idyllic past. There are, however, other sources that provide some knowledge about American quilts. One can develop socioeconomic studies based on inventory and probate records, which often indicate the presence, number, and relative value of quilts. A great many textiles were imported and many were relatively expensive, so quilts and other bedcoverings were listed separately. Although, unfortunately, these records give very little detail concerning color, style, or origin, another source, merchants' advertisements, provides an excellent indication of the variety of textiles available to the American of means, particularly in more established population centers. Family histories, diaries, the "reminiscences" of early settlers of small communities, and genealogical materials are all of major importance in documenting specific information about the quiltmakers and the geographic origin of textiles. (The quilts illustrated in this essay are all documented, as to maker and region.)

These sources show us that some quilts were made for purely utilitarian purposes, while others were especially made in a more decorative manner. It is quilts of the latter type that are generally found today in museums and private collections—the utilitarian examples have disappeared as a result of the use for which they were intended. Quiltmakers living in more populated areas were able to take advantage of better sources for fabrics, largely imported textiles, but between 1770 and 1880 the vast majority of American quilts were made in rural areas by women of the middle and lower classes.

There is ample evidence in the historical record that ready-made quilts imported from England were readily available in many of the more populated areas. For example, a review of advertisements in Virginia newspapers from 1770 to 1780 shows that in Gloucester, Williamsburg, Richmond, and Alexandria, it was possible to purchase Marseille quilting, cradle quilts, Persian quilts, and silk and satin quilts. The Industrial Revolution in England had created massive changes in the production of textiles, and spinning machines were also available in America, as detailed in *The Virginia Gazette* of January 17, 1777:

Whereas the mystery of SPINNING AND WEAVING is so very little known and so badly practiced, in this and all other parts of America, we the subscribers think proper to inform the publick what kind of goods we are capable of manufacturing, viz. Cottons of all sorts, jeans, pillows, thicksets, velvet, velveret, baragon jeans, calicoes, muslins, German, French, and common stripes, Dutch cords, corded dimities, corderoys, royal ribs, denims, satinets, Indian jeans, jennets, drawboys, quiltings. . . . We have also for sale SPINNING MACHINES, that will spin a pound in an hour of 8 yard thread, to work with any number of spindles. . . .

Fig. 1 Example of appliqué patch made by Mary Ann Barringer of Cabarrus County, North Carolina in early nineteenth century.

In the same advertisement, while extolling the many products that they are capable of manufacturing, the textile makers indicate that they may be called to any part of America "so that we shall always be ready and willing to do all we can for the good of the country."

Although city-dwellers might use imported textiles, the majority of the early one-piece quilts had rural origins. And often the wool tops, as well as the backings, are homespun. The quilt is composed of three layers, the top fabric being pieced together. The filling is usually a layer of wool for additional warmth. The entire quilt is decorated in an allover quilting pattern, usually in a large floral motif. The stitches, because of the thickness of the fabric, are usually not closely executed. Many of these quilts were cut away for the four-poster bed and would today be considered bedspreads. These early quilts may have been designed as imitations of the expensive imports seen in major metropolitan areas by those who could not afford to buy them.

Newspaper advertisements again directed to the more wealthy urban clientele indicate another early quilt form in America, the patchwork. Imported fabrics were available as appliqué patches, which could be stitched down to create a pleasing design. In *The Boston Evening Post* of October 13, 1760, Jonathan and John Amory announced that they had for sale "English and India Patches."[1] Later, block printer John Hewson made similar fabric pieces in Philadelphia. His bright, colorful birds, and flowers in urn-shaped vases, could be used to make an extremely decorative bed quilt.[2] (See Fig. 1 for examples of appliqué of

patches, made in a later generation, in a more rural area.) The bedcoverings produced with these purchased patches were expensive and highly ornamental; such quilts are now eagerly sought by collectors.

Baltimore album quilts, which were greatly influenced by Mrs. Achsah Goodwin Wilkins's "Marseille quilts," can be placed within this same urban context. Mrs. Wilkins used high-quality imported and purchased patches, as did the ladies of the Methodist Church of Baltimore, the later creators of the album quilts.[3]

One often fails to realize that quilting was considered a chore performed in addition to the myriad of other sewing tasks that women undertook during this period. A glimpse of one woman's life is provided by Mrs. Lucy Johnson Ambler, writing from Fauquier County, Virginia, in 1822:

I have put a bed quilt in frame and you know that must be a tedious job. The quilt was commenced by Mr. Ambler's mother and I think I am bound to finish it. Catherine and Elizabeth Ambler are staying with me and they occasionally assist me though not much. Besides this quilt I have another very serious job on hand which is working a spencer for myself which is a good deal for me to do as I do all the sewing for my family.[4]

Unfortunately, the quilt Mrs. Ambler mentioned has not survived, although a pieced quilt from another rural area of Virginia is illustrated here (Fig. 2). Rarely do the quilt and the written word exist together. The busy lives of these country

Fig. 2 This Star of Bethlehem—*illustrating the art of piecing—was made by Almedia Gibson Lumm of Mountville, Loudoun County, Virginia, about 1840.*

Fig. 3 Another example of innovative piecing is this strong, well-designed quilt made of wool scraps by Fannie Gatewood Grimes of Keysburg, Kentucky, in the late nineteenth century.

women usually precluded their discussing their everyday activities. Indeed, one must marvel at the copious correspondence of Mrs. Ambler when she faced so many other tasks.

Although quilting may have been taught in the women's educational institutions that began to flourish in late eighteenth-century America, there is little to indicate that the young ladies finished whole quilts. One student, Eliza Southgate of Medford, Massachusetts, writing from Susanna Rawson's School on January 9, 1798, did seem interested in piecing and designing:

> *Dear Father... You mentioned in your letter about my pieces which you say you imagine are purloined; I am very sorry they are for I set more by them than any of my pieces; one was the Mariner's Compass and the other was a Geometrical piece....* [5] [Fig. 3]

The same young woman later indicated in her correspondence to Moses Porter what her period of education had provided her:

> Sunday, Scarborough, May 1801
> *...I learned to flutter with a thoughtless gaiety—a mere feather which every breath had power to move. I left school with a head full of something, tumbled in without order or connection. I returned home with a determination to put it in more order.... But I soon lost all patience (a virtue I do not possess in any eminent degree), for the greater part of my ideas I was obliged to throw away without knowing where I got them or what I should do with them; what remained I pieced as ingeniously as I could into a few patchwork opinions,—they are now almost threadbare, and as I am about quilting a few more, I beg you will send me any spare ideas you may chance to have....* [6]

It is doubtful that Eliza Southgate and the many other young ladies who attended the fashionable boarding schools of the day, ever made any quilted bedcovers. The more economically well-off ladies could purchase their quilts ready-made or used alternative bedcoverings.

Although not technically a quilt, white-on-white remains a popular category within the American quilt-making tradition. Although it would be difficult to prove, one might suggest that these hand-executed white work examples were an attempt to copy the popular but more expensive machine-made Marseille quilting, which continued to be advertised and sold well into the nineteenth century. One should also recognize that the popularity of American-made white work coincides with the rise and development of the neoclassical style, about 1790 to 1840. In this period ancient Greek and Roman motifs were revived and copied as decorative elements on furniture, ceramics, glass, and silver. The use of pure white was symbolic of classical purity. The stuffed motifs on white work resembled the carvings on furniture of the period, just as the details on architectural

Figs. 4 and 4a White stuffed quilt (left), made by Orella Keiler Horton of Ridgefield, Connecticut, about 1825, and detail (above).

Fig. 5 Princess Feather appliqué, made by Louvisa Houchins of Illinois, shows one of the extremely popular patterns of the mid-nineteenth century.

Fig. 5a Detail of Princess Feather quilt.

decorative plasterwork are often reminiscent of this style. Among the typical motifs of white work are feathers, wreaths, cornucopias, baskets of flowers, and leaves (Figs. 4 and 4a). Areas not covered by the designs are generally stitched in closely spaced diagonal lines. Today the term "trapunto" is often used for this technique, although the word was never used in the early nineteenth century.

To make a stuffed bedcovering, only two fabrics were used. The top was a fine or plain-weave cotton, and the backing was a loosely woven cotton or muslin. A design was penciled or drawn on the backing and the two layers were stitched together, following the design. A sharp utensil was used to separate the backing fibers, creating a small hole. Cotton batting was inserted between the two layers into the various design motifs, making them stand out. Then the fibers on the backing were moved back to the original positions. (A hole was never cut in the backing.) Cording could be used for vines, and sometimes French knots and other embroidery enhanced the decoration of the top.

By mid-century local historians had begun to produce reminiscences. In these histories one finds many references to the immense popularity of quilting parties, which gave women in remote rural areas an opportunity for entertainment and interaction with friends and neighbors.

Quilting at that time [between 1768 and 1853], as now, was one of the practical amusements of the ladies in town; but the preparations which preceded a quilting party were much more extensive than at present, on account of the distance from which the inhabitants lived from each other, and the almost impassable state of the roads or paths. To attend a "quilting" at the more distant parts of the town, as it was the practice then, was an absence from home of no less than three days; the first of which was spent in going, the second in quilting, and the third was consumed in returning. A mother, before starting on one of these expeditions, was obliged to bake a sufficient supply for the family at home; and if she was so fortunate, or unfortunate, as to have the care of an infant, she was under the necessity of putting it out with the neighbors, to be nursed, till she should return.[7]

By the mid-nineteenth century, a variety of fabric designs and quilting styles were evident. Fabrics were more generally available. Both *appliqué* (the application of a cut fabric onto the top of the quilt) and *piecing* (the combination of many small fragments of fabric to form a design) were popular methods for making quilts. Many of the quilts surviving from this era are midwestern in origin—as the frontier moved west, the quilting tradition moved with it. Quilt patterns were often exchanged; names of patterns vary from one region to another. (Examples of work from this major period are shown in Figs. 5, 5a, and 6).

By the late 1850s, the popular women's magazine *Godey's Lady's Book and Magazine* included several patterns for patch-

Fig. 6 Album-style appliqué quilt made by Mary E. Mannakee, Montgomery County, Maryland; dated 1853.

Fig. 7 Crazy-quilted slumber throw of silk, made in 1887 by Mettie Mehitable Ware of San Rafael, California. Embroidery pattern for crazy quilts could be purchased or ordered. The irregular shapes are given visual order by their arrangement—in nine blocks—and by the border that acts as a frame.

work. These articles, with their romantic explanations, contribute to the present lore, mystery, or romance with old quilts, for until recently they were our only explanation, leaving us with a lack of serious scholarship in the area.

> What little girl does not recollect her first piece of patchwork, the anxiety for fear the pieces would not fit, the eager care with which each stitch was taken, and the delight of finding the bright squares successfully blended into the pretty pattern. Another square and another, and the work begins to look as if in time it might become a quilt; then, as the little girl grows up to young ladyhood, the blushes flit across her cheek when, as she bends over her sewing, grandmamma suggests that making patchwork is a sign of matrimonial anticipations; then the mother, exercising all her ingenuity to make a pretty quilt for the little occupant of the cradle, until we go forward to the old grandmother, who finds patchwork the finest work her aged eyes and trembling fingers will permit her to undertake. From the house of the rich mother who finds expensive silk sewed in pretty patterns, the choicest covering for her darling, to the poor hovel, where every rag is treasured to eke out the winter quilt for the little ones, we find patchwork.[8]

The author then discussed album quilts:

> ...a very pretty idea. A lady gives the size of the square she wishes to each of her lady friends, who are willing to contribute to her quilt. They make a square according to their own taste, putting a white piece in the centre, on which they write their name. Every lady's autograph adorns her own square. An old lady in Charlestown showed me one in which there were one hundred squares, and all the contributors excepting twelve were dead. The quilt itself belonged to her mother, and was more than sixty years old.[9]

Most album quilts date at the earliest from 1840 to 1850!

Later generations, particularly those who were more financially secure, turned to a more expensive but less durable fabric—silk—to create the crazy quilt (Fig. 7). Most crazy quilts date from the 1870s to about 1890. These colorful creations were not intended for use on a bed, but rather for show as a lap robe or "throw." A pamphlet of the period informed:

> As the name indicates, it is simply sewing odd scraps and bits of Silk, Satin, Plush, Pieces from cast-off neck-ware of gentlemen friends, old ribbons, samples of a friend's dresses, etc. (of which any size or shape can be used) in a 'haphazard' sort of way, so that the angles may somewhat imitate the craze of old china, from which all this kind of work derives its name.[10]

The same pamphlet, which cost twenty-five cents, instructed the reader on the proper fabrics, the foundation, and the decoration. All of the typical embroidery designs were illustrated—including the anchor, chains, top hat, fans, butterflies, spider and web, and flowers—as were all of the commonly seen decorated outline stitches. The author suggested that the maker save scraps; however, they could be easily obtained for sixty cents to one dollar from advertisers in the pages of *Peterson's Magazine*. While some crazy quilts are individualistic, incorporating souvenir memorabilia in the design, many are based on patterns that were available for copying from the popular ladies' magazines.

This brief history provides illustrations of the work of a few individuals. Later generations admired and cared for these quilts, and the textiles formed part of the family's heritage. In these instances, the documented quilts add greatly to our knowledge of the many now-forgotten women who quilted in early America.

NOTES

1. Susan Burrows Swan, *A Winterthur Guide to American Needlework*. New York: Crown Publishers, 1976, p. 112.

2. Ibid., pl. XV, p. 95.

3. Dena S. Katzenberg, *Baltimore Album Quilts*. The Baltimore Museum of Art, 1980.

4. "Letters from Mrs. Lucy Ambler to Mrs. Sally Ambler," *The Virginia Magazine of History and Biography* 23, January 1915: 188.

5. Eliza Southgate Bowne, *A Girl's Life Eighty Years Ago: Selections from the Letters of Eliza Southgate Bowne*. New York: Charles Scribner's Sons, 1888, p. 72.

6. Ibid., p. 83.

7. James C. Rice, ed., *The Secular and Ecclesiastical History of the Town of Worthington to 1853*. Albany, N.Y.: Weed, Parsons & Co., 1953, p. 17.

8. Ellen Lindsay, "Patchwork," *Godey's Lady's Book and Magazine* LV, February 1857: 166.

9. Ibid.

10. T. E. Packer, ed., *A Choice Collection of Ornamental Patches for Crazy Patchwork*. Boston: The Boston Herald, 1885.

The author wishes to express her gratitude to Michael Berry, Curator of Collections, DAR Museum, who extensively researched records at the Library of Congress to provide data on American quilt makers.

CHAPTER 2

GEOMETRY AND FLOWERS

MIRIAM SCHAPIRO

What is a quilt? Among other things, it is the history of women, a receptacle of passions, attitudes, largesse, and anger. It is a reassembling process, which in itself may embody a solution to human problems. It is inspiration, a connection with self, the dogged will to make something extraordinary in the midst of family routine, a sense of wholeness, the wish to please, to succeed, pleasure in the act of working and knowing the power of "making."

It is also discovering that making something beautiful heals exhaustion; it is finding what it is to be next to the stars.[1] And feeling mysterious forces that urge one on—impulses, starts, finishes, disappointments, reworkings (marking, setting, rolling, binding), washing, folding, bending over, discovering, refining.

Although quilts have their own special domain in the history of folk art and have constituted a universal form of needlework since before 1750, only now is their significance as an indigenous American art form created exclusively by women beginning to be recognized. The quilting tradition illuminates the darkness of women's history like a torch, showing us the strength and power of women as artist-makers and the consolidation of women as a sharing community.

While the darkness enveloped many women who strove to express themselves, the quiltmakers were fortunate. Theirs was an environment in which functional objects were life's blood. Intimate, limited, stable, and waiting, their audience never drifted away. A history of cold nights in unheated second stories for hundreds of years was the challenge, met by the production of more quilts than we can imagine. Not all quilts were good, nor all made with affection, but those that survive and come down to us as esthetic surprises have a sense of self-validation that in itself is a splendid heritage.

In the area of visual control, the quiltmakers, sometimes working on a field even larger than 103″ by 91″, demonstrated an impressive understanding of the language of form.[2] Their conception of order and geometry makes us remember women's earlier experiences cultivating the land. Eons ago, as hunting gave way to the domestic life separated from the kill, as the seasons acquired a new significance, women began to perceive themselves as those who would tame and provide for the interior landscape. They would move between anarchy and beauty. Seeds had been sown; cultivation symbolically entered a new form of life, which argued control and certainty.

Such a heritage led to high graphic consciousness, as among the Chilkit and Navajo women, whose ability to render ideas (religious, political, or simply visions of the physical world) in both concrete and abstract forms brought extraordinary beauty to familiar objects.

Standards of excellence immediately reveal themselves in quilts. It is easy to see the relationship between art and mathematics: from conceptualization on, the skilled needleworker must be in command of the precise ordering of stitch to stitch,

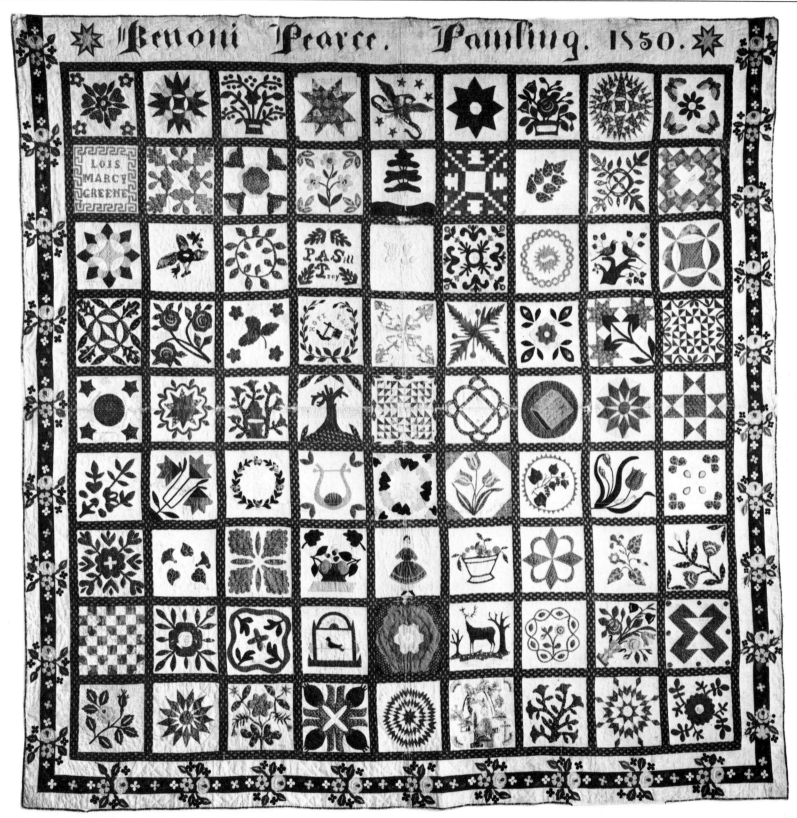

Pieced and appliquéd quilt, 103" x 103". Eighty-one squares made and signed by the relatives of Benoni Pierce of Pawling, New York.

Invitation, *Miriam Schapiro, 1982, acrylic and fabric collage, 90" x 144".*

piece to piece, or else the entire work will be chaotic, the grand design ruined.

Humans invented geometry for themselves. Pattern arranged in an enclosed space is divided and proportioned by geometry. In the counterchange between positive and negative shapes, we find the blueprint for endless variations on a theme. This is what the early quilters knew. There seems to be a knowing rhythm of information passed down, generation to generation, in which organic timing and formal rhyming exchange with each other in the language of form. Over the centuries, women taught these principles to their daughters; as the standards were set, meaning evolved both overtly and covertly.[3]

Besides the nonfigurative designs for quilts, there is another kind of pictorial image—a literal icon. Here, for example, a "house" is delineated and filled with fabric laid in the contour. The result is a clear house pictograph, part of an endless lexicon of forms: stork, baby in a crib, man, woman, dog, cat, horse, tree, flower, barn, schoolhouse, teacups, chair, bed, basket, scissors, spools, heart, hands, star, and fan.

These pictographic forms that comprise the iconography of quilts are arranged in a variety of ways. In many autobiographical quilts, there is a coming together of text, purpose, and presence that gives the work a special sense of wholeness. For example, in one family tree quilt, thirty-five blocks equal one branch of a family. The parents' names appear on the single blocks and the children's names on strips around the block. This kind of quilt was not made for use, but to be stored away— a legend of one's life—for posterity. It was signed, folded in tissue, recorded in the family Bible, and housed in a trunk in the attic.

The architectural basis of my own art reflects the measure of my hopes and dreams. How did the quiltmakers change my art? I had been a "pure" painter until I fell in love with quilts, but the story of my evolution is typical of what happened when fabrics became a metaphor for the quiet revolution. In the late 1960s I knew very little about the nature of fabrics, and nothing about their special history in women's culture. I never realized they could help me solve my painting problems, until I closed the gap between the "pure" studio and the everyday reality of my home. Once the doors to my outside studio were literally shut and I moved my painting materials back home, I learned from the quiltmakers how to do everything under one roof. I learned to add a new dimension to what I already knew: that even though painting indisputably raises a vivid image in the mind, quilts have a charismatic glow—so why not have the best of both worlds? I attached fabrics to my painted surfaces. After painting

Detail from Invitation.

a simple geometric structure, which served as a container for a burst of fabrics, I often glued sheer materials like printed chiffon over my acrylic scaffold. They appeared to flutter against the structure like a bird seeking freedom from the cage.

A decade has passed since those days, and many of us have reinvented ourselves as artists, as art historians, and as women. Taking a new look at history, we have found beauty in unexpected domestic sources. As a result, the sentient, sensual surface of our art has been changed by a profound involvement with the ideas and materiality found in quilts and other useful and decorative arts. The artist-makers of our past have become mentors for women who are now unafraid to see domestic life as a locus for the art-making process. For years now we have searched for old, memory-laden pieces of anonymous women's work that could be incorporated into new statements by gluing, sewing, photographing, or Xeroxing.[4] A renewed interest in the history of decoration recognizes that this element of design has from time immemorial been assigned to the world of women. In the 1970s, women artists demonstrated that "decorative was not a dirty word." For the first time in history, these women were "leaders" in a movement that inspired male artists as well. At this point in the 1980s, it is often difficult to tell men's fabric art or patterned art from women's.

Besides reviving quilts and quilt iconography, women artists also explored motifs of cultures past and present, remote and exotic, and added them to the contemporary vocabulary. Ornamentalism, the newest term for this resurgence of decorative vision, has affected architecture as well as painting, reminding us that the relationship between quilts and architecture is closer than that between quilts and painting, for both of the former provide utility as well as decoration.

Nonetheless, quilts must be accepted on their own terms, not measured against painting and architecture. If we were to remove them from the frame of reference of women's culture, we would obscure a unique aspect of their identity, and women would lose a significant element of their own history.

In the thirst for beauty, eyes and hands, servants of the imagination, translated primary forms into complex patterns. Delicate triangles started out as trees, massed into mountains, inverted to valleys, and recombined as forests—bordered by other triangles (whose shapes stayed geometric, as if there were no other use for them) appearing at measured intervals, in colors changing from sunshine to shadow. A mysterious shaping and reshaping formed in the luxury of the mind, where numberless images were stored like recipes, hoarded against a rainy day.

Notes

1. Titles of quilts are often descriptive, often poetic: *Stars and Planets*, *The Delectable Mountains*, *Star of the East*, *Passion Flower*, *Wheel of Fortune*, *Sunburst*, and so on.

2. There is an amazing variety of quilt types, such as Freedom, Memory, Friendship, Album, Bride, and crazy quilts.

3. In her book *Quilts, the Great American Art*, Patricia Mainardi is the first feminist to explain covert imagery in quilts.

4. I am indebted to Melissa Meyer for exploring women's culture with me in our collaborative article, "Waste Not/Want Not: Femmage," *Heresies* 4, 1978.

CHAPTER 3

UP, DOWN, AND ACROSS:
A New Frame for New Quilts

LUCY R. LIPPARD

It took me more than twenty years, nearly twenty-five, I reckon, in the evening after supper when the children were all put to bed. My whole life is in that quilt. It scares me sometimes when I look at it....I tremble sometimes when I remember what that quilt knows about me.
　　　　　　　　　　　—Anonymous nineteenth-century quiltmaker[1]

Quilts kind of filled in for the disappointment of not going to school to learn to be an artist.　　　　　　　　　　　—Anonymous quiltmaker[2]

Women have always made art. But for most women, the arts highest valued by male society have been closed to them for just that reason. They have put their creativity instead into the needlework arts, which exist in fantastic variety wherever there are women, and which in fact are a universal female art, transcending race, class and national borders.　　—Patricia Mainardi[3]

Since the new wave of feminist art began around 1970, the quilt has become the prime visual metaphor for women's lives, for women's culture. In properly prim grids or in rebelliously "crazy" fields, it incorporates Spider Woman's web, political networking, and the collage aesthetic. The purpose of this essay is to suggest a broad social framework for the perception of that metaphor, to stretch the frame within which "high" and "low" arts are perceived.

The quilt is a diary of touch, reflecting uniformity and disjunction, the diversity within monotony of women's routines. The mixing and matching of fragments is the product of the interrupted life. Quilts also incorporate the grid, a staple of women's art in the early days of the feminist art movement, symbolizing, perhaps, the desire to salvage order from domestic and other distractions. What is popularly seen as "repetitive," "obsessive," and "compulsive" in women's art is in fact a necessity for those whose time comes in small squares. Passive house*keeping* differs from active home*making*. Overdecoration of the home and "inherent female fussiness" can also be attributed to creative restlessness. Women are raised with an exaggerated sense of detail, which extends from body to house to the objects it contains. The need to be "busy" is often engendered by isolation within a particular space and by an ingrained emphasis on duty, cleanliness, and service.

On a historical level, the quilt can be seen as a symbol of the feminist resurrection of our foremothers' lives. As Louisiana sculptor Lucille Reed put it, "I have consciously used the elements of my maternal aunt's folk art. My work has gained in vitality from this recycling of my own heritage. The symbol of renewal of life in the use of discarded materials and the recurring symbol of the swollen form of expectant life are the threads that run through the different phases of my work."[4] Similarly Rosemary Wright, working with ten of her Mitchell relatives in this project, made a florally exploding pyramidal mountain of her family history, to commemorate the death of her mother.

Rehabilitation has always been woman's work. Necessity is the mother, not the father, of invention. The homemaker's touch is as often determined by economics as by biology. Patching, turning collars and cuffs, trimming and remaking old clothes, changing buttons to give a cheap dress more style, refurbishing furniture—these are the private resorts of the economically deprived woman to give her family public dignity. As Pattie Chase put it, "A woman made utility quilts as fast as she could so her family wouldn't freeze, and she made them as beautiful as she could so her heart wouldn't break."[5] The patchwork quilt originated in the careful patching of treasured antiques brought from the old countries. The crazy quilt—the most "liberated" of traditional styles—was originally the most pedestrian, using every available scrap for warmth. Ironically, when the crazy quilt became a fad at the end of the century, it was made only in the finest satins, silks, and velvets. Today in affluent Western societies, even outside the counterculture, expensive new clothes are made to *look* rehabilitated, and the quilt itself is as often found on the wall as on the bed—a victim of gentrification.

In a similarly paradoxical development, quilting (along with crocheting, rug-hooking, and needlepoint) came back into middle-class and upper-class fashion in the 1970s, in part on the apron strings of feminism. What was once women's *work* has been transformed into a pastime for the well-off and has become a "minor art" or "high craft." A number of quilt exhibitions have been held in fine art museums in the last decade. Whereas Navajo blankets, also made by women, have been so lauded for their geometric precision and influence on male abstract painters that they have acquired some mythical androgyny, quilts at least cannot be disguised as genderless. For that reason, however, and because they are the familiar products of our own culture rather than of some exotic and romanticized "other," quilts are unjustly seen as less bold and strong, more "feminine."

One of the new feminist emblems is Sheila de Bretteville's famous *Pink* poster of 1974—a collaboration of visual and verbal musings on the color by women of varying ages and backgrounds, modeled on the quilting grid. De Bretteville remarked that "the organization of material in fragments, multiple peaks rather than a single climactic moment, has a quality and rhythm which may parallel woman's ontological experience, particularly her experience of time." She says of quilts that they are "assemblages of fragments generated whenever there is time, which are in their method of creation as well as in their aesthetic form, visually organized into many centers. The quilting bee, as well as the quilt itself, is an example of an essentially non-hierarchal organization."[6] It has often been noted that quilting bees were as much social as utilitarian events—antidotes to rural isolation, times when women could get together and share news, recipes, patterns. They were political meetings, too. Support for women's suffrage was certainly "networked" over quilts. Susan B. Anthony's first public demand for equal rights was raised at a quilting bee, an event appropriately commemorated by a runner for Anthony's setting in Judy Chicago's *Dinner Party*.

Crucial to the consideration of quilts, new and old, are the issues of skill and audience. The makers both of high culture (fine art) and low culture (crafts, folk art, commercial art, hobbies) are conditioned to know their audiences. High art is firmly contained by and channeled to a national and international, middle- and upper-class educated group; crafts and hobbies have a much more *local* audience, often commercially determined, presumably more restricted—but in fact they sometimes appeal to a broader audience than those who visit galleries and museums. What interests me is the hybrids that happen in the interstices, the art that rejects or avoids these narrow lanes. "The Artist and the Quilt Project" creates such hybrids by guiding "high artists" (those acknowledged in the art world) into

33

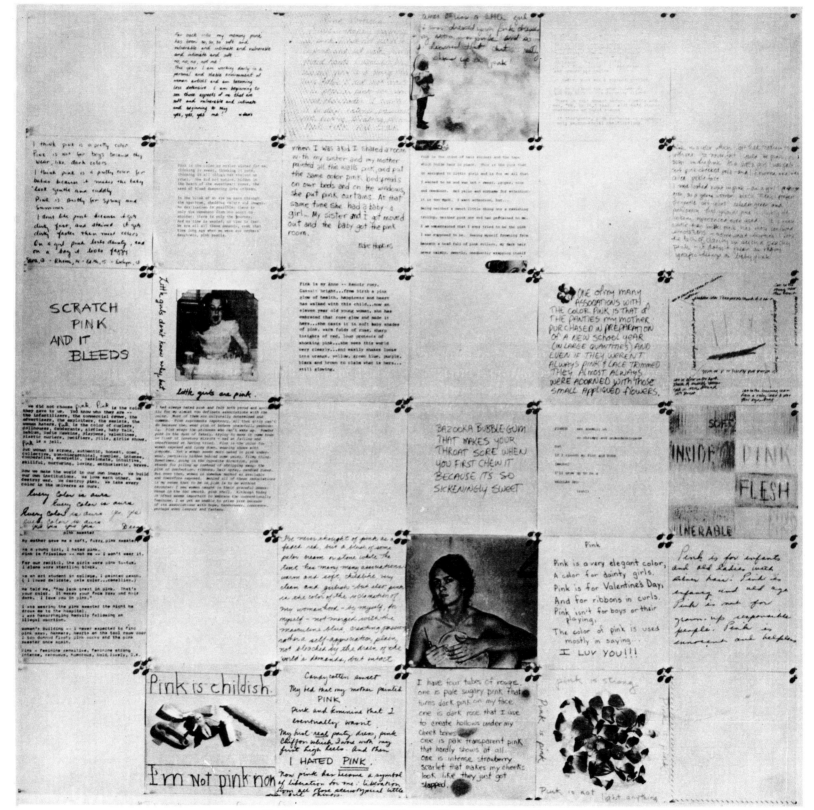

Pink (poster), Sheila de Bretteville, 1974, 19" x 19".

Runner for Susan B. Anthony's place setting from Judy Chicago's Dinner Party.

collaboration and "low culture," and guiding craftspeople (though not all the women who did the quilting here see themselves that way) into collaboration and "high culture."

Distinctions between "high" and "low" culture, amateur and professional, are usually used to exclude minorities, the lower classes, and women from full creative participation. Though art in general is something most people would like to like, contemporary mainstream art is not accessible, even physically, to many people. Modernist art has a history of alienating its cultured audience by being vulgar, and its vulgar audience by saying it is not cultured enough to understand. Progressive feminist artists are still trying to find a visual form and content that will meet the needs of all those people who are unsatisfied or untouched by what *is* available to them—a form that will meet the artists' needs, too. It shouldn't be such a radical idea to conceive of art as an empathetic exchange between artist and audience, a collaboration in communication where process is as important as product. Yet the whole hierarchy of low to high craftspeople and low to high graphic artists is based on relationships among producer, receiver, and object that the art world rarely acknowledges. The history of the quilt informs these divisions, which are, after all, products both of class and gender separation, and of the degree of economic support for the art in question. There are many crossings and contradictions. For instance, if high artists were only those people who could support themselves by their art, not many would qualify. And, on the other hand, if all who did support themselves by their art were called high artists, *Artforum* would be quite another magazine.

At this point, some questions have to be asked, if not necessarily answered: What kinds of skills are acceptable as Art and what are not, within our dominant culture? Says who? Who has access to the skills considered necessary to make art? Who does the artist think her audience is? How much control does she have over choosing and reaching that audience? Do these commissioned quilts become high art, thereby losing their populist appeal? Do they become low art, thereby losing their elitist appeal? Or do they (as I hope) have a chance of becoming something that subverts these imposed and divisive categories, something "uncategorizable," through the artists' reluctance to give way to such social restrictions? Of course these questions apply to each woman's work in different ways, but in a broader context, they raise another question: Why is the high/low or fine arts/crafts dichotomy there at all, and what social needs do such divisions fulfill?

Looking at the extraordinary manifestations of women's traditional arts in all cultures, one wonders what illogic led to the

Moby Dick, *Ann Wilson, 1955, synthetic polymer and cloth, 66¼" x 84".*

non-utilitarian object's becoming more valuable than the utilitarian. Of course, there's luxury and surplus value and so forth. By now it is easy to speculate with Marx that with the rise of capitalism, ownership came to rest with one class while use value came to rest in another, and that the useless acquired value through this association. (Thus the upward mobility of "Sunday best" arts—teacups or quilts, like clothes, used only on special occasions.) One factor in the perception of women's arts as "minor" must be the way they were wrenched from their initial cultural context and forced into comparison with larger-scale, more expensively constructed and socially respected men's work. Writing in 1859, novelist Dinah M. Craik reflected the prevailing assumptions:

> Art is the most difficult—perhaps, in its highest form, almost impossible to women.... All who leave domestic criticism to plunge into the open arena of art ... must abide by art's severest canons. One of these is, that every person who paints a commonplace picture ... contributes temporarily ... to lower the standard of public taste.... I would advise every woman to examine herself and judge herself, morally and intellectually, by the sharpest tests of criticism before she attempts art ... and be satisfied that the smallest achievement is nobler than the grandest failure.[7]

Quilts, because they are useful, inspire less fear in their makers of being time-wasters, selfish, or self-indulgent; they involve no confusion about the pretensions of Art. Accepted on their own modest terms, the context in which they were made also works against them, because of the reversed value system of "useful/useless." Artist/quiltmakers seeking aesthetic dignity now, as then, are caught in a queasy balance between tradition and modernism. Before the recent surge of feminism, few ambitious women artists on the New York art scene would have been caught dead making a quilt. Today they still dance a fine line. The prejudice against cooperative or collaborative art continues, unless high technology is involved. These recent quilts are, like most of their traditional predecessors, individually *conceived* and collaboratively *executed.* They remain, for better or worse, individual works of art, along the lines of Chicago's *Dinner Party* and her current, more flexibly organized *Birth Project,* where the artist/designer was helped by others, but approved all the final decisions.

The first quilt paintings I recall seeing were Anne Wilson's from the 1950s. After feminism opened the floodgates of women's history and the quilt became such a multifaceted symbol for women's culture, a number of artists reestablished their ties with women's traditional or amateur arts, scrutinizing the quilt and other needlework forms for new aesthetic as well as social meanings. In the Women's Art Registry of slides, begun in 1971,

Floorpiece VI, *Harmony Hammond, 1973, painted cloth, approximately 60" diameter.*

the form, the materials, and the patterns of traditional quilts began to appear frequently. Sometimes the materials were unexpected; I recall one "quilt" made of crushed cola cans, one of ceramic, others of plastic or metal. Photographer Amy Stromsten photo-silkscreened her quilt, and in 1976 Joan Lyons made a stunning artist's book in which each page has a quilted texture and is illustrated by a quilt square; the text consists of a 1925 letter/memoir from Abby Rogers to her granddaughter, about her own mother's silk patchwork quilt. The letter leads from quilt to home to school, echoing the form of the quilt itself, and the bits of lives it incorporated.

In 1973 Harmony Hammond made some brilliantly colored "floor pieces," which were in fact circular hooked rugs made of rags partially painted. These could be seen as ironic comments on then fashionable male abstract floor sculptures; they also deliberately flaunted their connection with the homely doormat, while "passing" as fine art. Hammond has always worked with rags and found fabrics, often remnants of friends' clothes; she

has done weaving and tailoring, and her fantasy personages consist of fans, ruffles, and braid—all of which she has incorporated into her quilt with Bob Douglas for this project, along with colors based on traditional Amish quilting.

Other artists in the project have taken innovative license with convention while successfully remaining within the quilt tradition. Ellen Lanyon and Angela Jacobi's lovely and traditionally detailed flower design peels away to parallel the layered quality of quilting, and refers to the process of making by the unfinished squares that blow around the top. Dorothy Gillespie and Bonnie Persinger humorously elongate their quilt, leaving it to fold on into space, as though depicting the time it took to make. Charlotte Robinson and members of the research staff, with a grid of hands, fused execution and image, making the hand a symbol of identity and presence as prehistoric peoples did. Marcia King and Nancy Vogel's terry cloth "brushstrokes" refer to King's paintings. Such cross-pollination of media is also evident in the work of Isabel Bishop (with Wenda F. von Weise),

Charlotte Robinson (with Bonnie Persinger), and Alice Neel (with Chris Edmonds), who actually translated paintings into quilts; so did Betty Parsons (with Amy Chamberlin), though her interlocking geometric shapes share more with the basic quilt form. Robinson's work went through three stages; from painting, to quilt, to painting over quilt.

In ancient Peru, the weaving of textiles was sacred, performed as a ceremonial art; the products defined differences in rank. The American quilt, on the other hand, originated from the other end of the economic scale. As Alice Walker wrote about a unique quilt picturing the Crucifixion, which now hangs in the Smithsonian Institution, attributed to "an anonymous Black woman in Alabama a hundred years ago": "If we could locate this 'anonymous' Black woman from Alabama, she would turn out to be one of our grandmothers—an artist who left her marks in the only materials she could afford and in the only medium her position in society allowed her to use."[8]

Fanny Moore, an ex-slave from North Carolina, recalled, "My mammy, she work in the field all day and piece and quilt all night. Then she has to spin enough thread to make four cuts for the white folks every night. Why sometimes I never go to bed. Have to hold the light for her to see by. She have to piece quilts for the white folks too."[9] After slavery, black women were still forced by poverty to sell their finest work for pittances.[10] Slave quilts have been traced back to the appliqué work of the Congo/Angola areas from which most American slaves were kidnapped. Many quilters inventively incorporated African and Native American motifs, as contemporary artists also do with impunity. Faith Ringgold's Harlem quilt for this project, made with her mother—dress-designer Willi Posey—bears an indirect resemblance to a Couples Quilt made by Mary Jane Batson from her mistress' ballgowns in mid-nineteenth-century Virginia.

The most overtly social patchworks being made today are the Chilean *arpilleras*—pictures made by women collectively from remnants found outside factories. Smuggled out of the country, they memorialize sons, husbands, and loved ones who have "been disappeared," and help maintain resistance against the fascist junta. Their narrative tone ranges from hope to despair, but, like North American traditional quilts, they employ bright color and lively form—not to belie the pain but to transcend it, to lend strength for endurance.

Several quilts in this project pay homage to third-world cultures. Mary Beth Edelson and Marie Ingall's proudly rising woman is bordered by stark motifs that could be Native American or African. Betye Saar and Judy Mathieson's piece evokes something Asian, with its lyrically floating fans, hearts, hankies.

Joyce Kozloff, pioneer of the so-called pattern painting movement, has long perused the decorative traditions of Islam and Mexico, among others, for her paintings, drawings, books, and tiled public architectural works; her quilt was made with Patricia Newkirk. Lynda Benglis's quilt is derived from Indian kites and lush Indian fabrics; quilter Amy Chamberlin got into the spirit and added "outrageous touches" of glittering gold thread and imagistic stitching.

Progressive artists find fertile ground today in regional, ethnic, labor, women's histories—all the lost stories of the disenfranchised. Miriam Schapiro, who worked with Marilyn Price, is an expert at resurrecting patterns from the past and transforming them into striking contemporary works without losing the flavor of their roots. Alice Baber and Edith Mitchell's quilt is traditional in appearance, but then reveals an elegant, unfolding floral form. Elaine Lustig Cohen's geometric abstraction painting style lent itself perfectly to the quilt form, merging—rather than merely reflecting—the arts of two times into an authentic collage; her quilt was made with Sharon McKain. Marilyn Lanfear and daughter Theresa Helms took the notion of a traditional Marriage Quilt and rent it asunder in an ironic modern assessment of the institution, thus simultaneously commenting on artistic and social tradition.

The introduction of dominant art-world values into a craft-oriented form or community is a double-sided situation. Despite good intentions, it can be condescending and counterproductive (witness the feelings reported by a few quilters in this project); or it can provide the seeds of a genuinely motivated creativity emerging from the grassroots of women's own lives and environments. The discontinuity between expectations and needs, between the realities of public and artist, is a crucial issue in attempts to leap the "high–low" barriers. It has to be understood in the historical context of "deskilling," begun during the Industrial Revolution, when the homemade and the rural were devalued and not replaced by any cohesive new urban culture, thereby intensifying class differences and permitting the powers that be to control and change the nature of craft or folk art. Arnold Hauser made an important point when he noted that the producers and consumers of folk art are "hardly distinguishable from each other," whereas the "hits" of mass culture have come from "professional upperclass writers who remained linked to their class."[11]

Increased specialization is what keeps capitalism going. It has led to fragmentation of experience and homogenization of culture. When the factory worker became ashamed of the homemade rug and spent her factory-earned money to buy the more expensive factory-made goods she'd also made herself, the gap

Couples Quilt, Mary Jane Batson, mid-nineteenth century, Richmond, Virginia, pieced and appliquéd cotton, 74" x 80". Batson, who was a slave, pieced the squares. After the Civil War she gave them to her granddaughter, Maria Chapman, who completed the quilt during the 1870s. Collection of Ron and Marcia Spark.

Heaven and Hell, *anonymous Chilean woman, 1970s,* arpillera *(patchwork painting).*

Craftwork, *Margaret Harrison, 1980, actual object, photograph, and painting.*

between minor and major arts widened. British artist Margaret Harrison made this the subject of a 1980 installation utilizing items owned by her working-class mother-in-law. Her *Craftwork* demonstrated deskilling in objects ranging from lovely old handmade patchwork to partially handworked needlework to factory-made doilies, and commented on their respective "quality."

"The Artist and the Quilt Project" shares with the community arts and even some New Wave neighborhood collectives a need to examine and close artificial gaps between high and low culture, to reintegrate art and social life. Within the context of feminist opposition to patriarchal values and to the colonization/destruction of other cultures, the quilt form offers a provocative vehicle for outreach. The new hybrids (these quilts could be an early stage) are in a sense collages of previous art attitudes. Raymond Williams's terms, "residual, dominant, and emergent cultures," are helpful here. "Residual" would be the history of the quilt—the stubborn legacy of "anonymous" women from all our pasts; "dominant" would be the component by which art is now defined and which makes *these* contemporary quilts verge on high culture, while others do not, because the women who made these have names, even "big names." And the "emergent" element is part of a *re*skilling process that involves social change as well as *exchange*—a major factor in the development of a cultural democracy.

Only a few feminist art groups in the United States have reached out directly to interact with non–art-world women making quilts and other traditional arts. One of the most positive aspects of "The Artist and the Quilt Project" is the way it provides a context for craftswomen to see themselves as artists, to understand the broader application of the word. On the other hand, a disturbing aspect reflects what the word *artist* has come to mean; rugged individualism fuels competition, divides women as it divides men, and inspires new fears.

The audience for feminist art is still mostly contained within the middle-class, museum-going art audience. "The Artist and the Quilt Project," like *The Dinner Party*, which pioneered the resurrection of needlework and cooperation between artists and craftswomen, will probably draw many women who do not consider themselves particularly interested in art. But so far there have been few attempts outside of the community arts movement to destroy the class-based barriers between "hobbyists," "craftswomen," and "artists."[12] More communication through state fairs, rural crafts classes, community centers, churches, union halls, and art galleries might encourage a truly innovative *art of making* that would transcend these barriers and acknowledge function as one function of art.

NOTES

1. Quoted in Margaret Ickis, *The Standard Book of Quilt Making and Collecting*. New York: Dover Publications, 1960, p. 270.

2. Quoted in Allen H. Eaton, *Handicrafts of New England*. New York: Bonanza Books, 1969, p. 341.

3. Patricia Mainardi, "Quilts: The Great American Art," *The Feminist Art Journal*, 2, no. 1, Winter 1973, pp. 1, 18–23.

4. Lucille Reed, in flyer for Wyly Tower Gallery, Ruston, LA, n.d (mid-1970s).

5. Pattie Chase, "Quilting: Reclaiming Our Art," *Country Women*, no. 21, Sept. 1976, p. 9.

6. Sheila de Bretteville, quoted by Deena Metzger, "In Her Image," *Heresies*, no. 2, May 1977, p. 5.

7. Dinah M. Craik, *A Woman's Thoughts about Women*. New York: Rudd & Carleton, 1859, pp. 50–53.

8. Alice Walker, "In Search of Our Mother's Gardens," Ms. magazine, May 1974, p. 54.

9. Fanny Moore, quoted in Judy Chicago and Susan Hill, *Embroidering Our Heritage: The Dinner Party Needlework*. Garden City, NY: Anchor Press/Doubleday, 1980, p. 222.

10. C. Kurt Dewhurst, Betty MacDowell, and Marsha MacDowell, *Artists in Aprons*. New York: E. P. Dutton in association with the Museum of American Folk Art, 1979, p. 55. This book has been a valuable source for the present essay. The richest other lode I found was "Women's Traditional Arts: The Politics of Esthetics," *Heresies*, no. 4, Winter 1978.

11. Arnold Hauser, quoted by J. Hoberman, "In Defense of Pop Culture: Love and Death in the American Supermarketplace," *The Village Voice/Literary Supplement*, no. 12, Nov. 1982, p. 11.

12. The best source of information on what progressive and the community arts movement is doing is *Cultural Democracy*, published by NAPNOC, P.O. Box 11440, Baltimore, MD 21239.

CHAPTER 4

BREAKING STARS:
A Collaboration In Quilts

ELEANOR MUNRO

I've seen a strange thought attributed to Goethe, although I can't find it in his famous book on optics. Perhaps it comes from a poem. *Color is the pain of light.* Thinking about quilts, I found myself returning to the line. It seemed to say something both accurate and suggestive about this art medium. For more than any other category of work, I think, the quilt is an amalgam of color and life experience. And experience might well be called the pain of Being.

The analogy is easy to draw. As light breaks into the spectrum of colors, so each person's first condition of being—one in the unity of a family—is shattered. To put it in biblical or symbolic terms, we break with each "paradise" or point of origin. Then, as we learn to distinguish objects in the field of colors that is the visible world, so we learn humanity in a field of experience. The purple, green, and yellow of the human condition are people and events experienced, then lost from their matrix in our lives. And the quiltmaker's mission, whether she lived two hundred years ago or yesterday, whether she is conscious of it or not, is to rescue those people and moments from oblivion, just as much as it is to fit the colorful swatches of cloth on her table into a design.

In this labor, the quiltmaker shares in the larger labor of all creative people. The will to form is a gift of grace beyond categories of sex. However, since in the past most women were without worldly power, they exercised this will in domestic projects that bore only metaphoric relationship to projects on the wider scene. Making a quilt was, then, such a metaphoric

work of proud, synthesizing vigor. "There is a world of suffering in that quilt," I've heard it said, and that says it all. The drive has been purposeful: patch by patch to reformulate unities that antedated the painful coming-apart. To me, the most moving quilt pattern of history, in this respect, is the *Broken Star.* I admire it for its visual majesty, which reinforces the meaning I read in it. Often I wonder how it came to some woman's mind that to set eight white squares on a colorful starburst would be to "break" that star.[1] Then I decided she was reversing the Goethean idea, saying that color could be imploded back into the unity and peace of white from which it came. It that case she would have been anticipating Malevich by some one hundred fifty years at least and would, like the Russian, have been expounding a subtle mysticism. But many such yearning thoughts must have impelled the nameless women who had to experience the dismembering of their families during the past century of migrations of peoples so that, one by one, they gave their quilts names that lift our own imaginations: *Flying Cloud, Wonder of the World, Ship's Wheel.*

With beautiful structural instinct, these early seamstresses, seeking to rise in their minds to a position from which the fragmented nature of human life could be gathered up in a wider vision, laid claim to this particular object, the coverlet, necessary in all households, on which to lavish their skill and their idealism. Myth and psychology affirm that that process of attaining a higher consciousness, as earlier, of entering life itself, entails a breaking of some kind. So here again is expressed the connection between the loss of an original intact state and the forming of the quilt. For the basic thing about historic quilt art was that it was bed art. The Marriage Quilt was a work of art whose deep purpose was to shelter and consecrate the sexual act, the beginning of the bridal pair's sexual life and so maturity, and their entry into the flow of history. That quilt was an offering at a sanctified site, a small enclosure on the curve of earth where the profane and instantaneous met the timeless and sacred. There, the single act merged and was lost in the coupling of generations. This artwork bore witness not to a limited sensual gratification, but to the taking on of life's whole burden.

Along the way, the very making of that quilt would work upon the adolescent initiate into the mysteries of adulthood. Slow, methodical, intricately detailed, its preparation would provide a steadying rhythm as the girl grew toward readiness for motherhood. With gravity and growing capability, she would be conducted, step by step, toward her great turning point. According to some traditions, she would sew a dozen quilt-tops before she met her future mate. The thirteenth she would start while she was making up her mind, and by the time it was done, if all went well, she would be engaged. That would, of course, be the Engagement Quilt, and her friends who helped quilt it would also sign it. Then, while the marriage plans were being made, the twelve earlier tops would be unpacked from the hope chest, stretched one by one on the quilting frame, and brought to

completion. Festive evenings would be spent and a mammoth quilting bee would cap the proceedings, only to be capped in turn by the wedding itself. Then, under the *Broken Star, Feather Star, Ozark Star*, under the *Star of Hope* or *Starry Lane*[2] would be enacted the ritual old as life, which the innocent bride must have hoped would be consummated with at least as much grace as she had already brought to the making of the cover. And later would come quilts for the births of children and other family milestones.

During the years to come, if there was a playful side to the collecting of the quilt scraps—somebody's necktie and somebody else's petticoat—there was also a more intangible "saving" going on. Retrieving, sorting, choosing, piecing—these acts stood fiercely against the condition poet Louise Glück described in a poem about a woman for whom "the waste's my breakfast." The sad thing about a lost life is that its constituent experiences have been left unassembled by the mind that lived them. With the accumulation of fragments of cloth, those fragmented events were given some permanence.

Moreover, the making of a quilt, which at one point in the life-span celebrated marriage, was also a response of strength to the fact of death. I've read of infants buried in tiny coffins lined with quilts made of their baby clothes. Could there be a greater labor of refusal-of-despair than that sewing? Faith Ringgold's grandmother made such a quilt to keep the memory of an infant boy alive. And if quilt-making preceded such events as a house-warming, it also preceded, to negate the "waste" of, such events as a family's departure from a community or a man's retirement. The quilter's hands and eyes, perhaps even without the collaboration of her conscious intelligence, understood that she was engaged in a process of creation that, as much as literal birth, brought into being a vehicle of human continuity. The redemption of those memory-laden bits from the random dispersal that is the sign of decay: that was what gave the art of the quilt, in the past, its latent religious character.

The word "religious" has overtones of binding-up and connecting, once upon a time with the gods of the sky. On a superficial level, then, what more "religious" art could there be than this one literally bound up by thread? But on a deeper level, it's remarkable how many of the old motifs come straight from the worldwide repository of religious symbols that mediate between the ground and the upper air. For example, such patterns as *Winged Square*, the various *Baskets*, and *Apple Tree* incorporate perfect yantras, the symbol of female and male powers in the universe, according to Hindu belief. The yantra is composed of intersecting triangles representing the Goddess and her spouse (how comical then, and also a little sad, that the pattern called *Old Maid's Puzzle* shows the proper triangles pointing up and down but never quite making contact).

So too the very labor applied to the quilt must have exercised a "religious" influence on the quilter. When she picked one pattern—after examining the materials she had at hand, taking account of her physical state (virgin, pregnant, newly delivered, and so on through life) and the time available to her (say, a long winter ahead)—she would thereafter give herself up to it and live for a while in its spell. Every day she would bring herself, anew, to concentration on its geometry. It might even enter her dreams at night, as an Eastern mystic dreams her or his mandala. Indeed, a woman making *Apple Tree* might be said to be "making her mandala" every time she sat down to work, to cut the triangles, smooth them, lay them in place on the table. No wonder a sense of special contentment is reported even by today's quiltmakers. "It's like praying," says one woman.

It would be difficult to know the full range of feelings and hopes that motivated the sixteen quilters in this present-day project. But it seems significant that several of them joined the collective during a time when their marriages were breaking up. Perhaps there is still something to the idea that, in going back and forth between a shaky world and a stable quilting frame, the woman feels herself assume new power, if not to change her fate, to accept it.

Also, every quilter in this project was aware of doing work her ancestors had done and so felt strengthened by community. Harold Rosenberg once wrote that "folk art stands still. It neither aspires upward like academic painting nor advances forward like the inventions of the modernist art movements." The traditional quilter, with her cloth, dyes, thread, needles, frames, is embedded in reminders of tradition, and in that sense "stands still," among her forebears. Yet among the sewing company here represented are many who also have the aspiration of the modernist artist, and so have consciously tried to push their work upward and forward.

This fact leads us to the actual circumstances of this project as it was kept on the tracks over seven years, much through the initiative of artist Charlotte Robinson. The original idea was that "artists" would design and "quilters" render the works. Some artists had long been involved with feminist ideas and, thus, sewing techniques; others, not at all. The range of design types is wide. I've divided them into categories by the look of them: Those in Category I look most like traditional quilts; those in Category V, least. What essential "quilt-ness" then survives the transition from "folk" to "signature" art? To begin with, the functional purpose is changed: these are, in actuality, wall hangings, and only theoretically coverlets. Also, the phenomenology of the "scrap pile," with its overtones of resurrection of clothes lived in and outgrown, has given way to the phenomenology of the artist's palette. These pairs of workers sought materials in shops, looking for colors and textures to fit preconceived programs. But the essence remains. These contemporary quilts, all of them, are instruments for the re-embodying of things, people, land- and skyscapes seen by the artists, held in their memories but lost in time.

Were the quilters then no more than artisans rendering in cloth other people's works of imagination? That was not at all the case in the collaborations that were most fruitful. In these instances, genuine translation took place. What was essential in the design was distilled out of it, and rethought in cloth terms. Isabel Bishop talked about this delicate subject. She noted that the fundamental thing in both painting and quiltmaking—indeed in any art—is *materiality*: perhaps only implicit in the first medium, but explicit in the second. To make a true translation, the quilter must be free to rethink the design in its *material* terms, not just as a presented image. In Bishop's case, the image was of girls walking. Now, any workhorse could copy and stamp that picture onto cloth. But quilter-artist Wenda von Weise brought her own intelligence to the problem, broke up the image and gave it authentic reincarnation via a photo-process of her own invention that uses color separations and color screens. The process, like Bishop's own use of transparent glazes, depends on the manipulation of light, the fracturing, we could say, of light into its constituent colors: a process, incidentally, uncannily appropriate for this subject, "quilt." In sum, collaboration is an art in itself. Like the generating of colors out of light, it is achieved only by breaking the original concept into parts, each part being a perspective on it by one individual. That much was learned, sometimes uncomfortably, during the years of this project.

We know that meaning, in all authentic contemporary art, resides in material and method, not only in image. Would I discover, I wondered at first, in the to-me unfamiliar language of cloth that same psycho-esthetic content one finds in paint, clay, and stone? The positive answer came in unanticipated ways. I'll take the case of one artist. She had made her mock-up and set out to find the right fabrics. She visited many stores and found many samples that appealed, but as many gave her a feeling of uneasiness. She reacted with particular anxiety to fabrics in which the fiber crossings were knotty and visible. Further, she recoiled from the juxtaposition of certain fabrics, such as silk and velvet, or from the use of certain stitches over velvet that crushed its nap. She searched and finally fell on the right material, a tight, smooth raincoat poplin, not precisely what one would think of for a bedcover. But she found it "useful...and with that, the whole quilt fell into shape. When I saw that poplin, I knew I had found something *timeless*."

Some cloth-workers might know what "timeless" means in terms of woven material, but I was not one, and I had to think about it. That led me back to what the artist had earlier told me about her childhood home. Central to it was her father, who suffered from a degenerative disease and in time became bedridden. What was happening in a medical sense was that nerve fibers meant to carry electrical impulses were becoming impassable. In her childish perception of his state, this artist had internalized the phenomenon of being "locked in" (the actual words she used of the distasteful fabrics). When she eventually became an artist feeding on memories of internal states for motivation, it was that original state of feeling she came back to. The call to design a quilt, an object to be laid, however theoretically, on a bed, pushed her into a dramatic, if disguised, reconfrontation with the painful scene that lay at the foundation of her mental life.

In the same way, a flow of awareness or empathy exists between every artist and the materials with which she works, endowing them with projected life. In that field, she will struggle continually to find her own shape in the multitudinous feeling-laden images that fill her mind. Such is the pressure under which the contemporary artist lives. Baber's petals of color unfolded above a black vortex, Benglis's kite-skies, Kozloff's gridded wall, Gillespie's rolling track of white down which flares of blue and yellow come plunging...these solutions to an assigned project ("design a quilt") are as revealing of personality as are the artists' works in more formal media, and as revealing as *Broken Star* of the meaning of "quilt" as a work of art. Saar's floating fans reminiscent of their vanished possessors, Wright's family mementos, Ringgold's neighbors' faces, Robinson's satellite's-eye view of a vast riverbed...these, like King's and Lanfear's conceptual works, are, as much as *Flying Cloud*, instruments for negating corrupting earthbound time.

Recently, while doing other projects and keeping an energizing correspondence with the members of this group, Charlotte Robinson has executed a series of large drawings of the hands of her artist friends. That series inspired the quilt seen on the cover of this book. Here are the hands of the collaborating artists—designers and quilters together. Their separate lives now have been permanently joined in this construct. There is a feminist message in this ghost-cloth of hand prints, of course: that women lost in time and anonymity are called back into being in the work of their daughters. But there is a more ancient and universal message here, too. For these hands are raised in the gesture that printed itself in paleolithic caves and prints itself today on house-walls in Africa, the Middle East, and Asia.

The gesture has several meanings. It says, Save me. Pain and evil pass me by. Lord God protect my children. But it also says simply, Remember me.

NOTES

1. Is it possible this marvelous pattern comes all the way from the North Transept Rose Window of Chartres Cathedral? That design has twelve rocking squares containing the Kings of Judah, Christ's ancestors, set around a central "star" containing Mary and Jesus. On black ground these jewel-bright geometries do indeed let light break through. Is it possible that Anonymous, who created the quilt pattern, had access to engravings of Gothic art?

2. There are hundreds of "star" patterns, more than any other category, and several of the works in the present collection also show stars as central motif or disguised template.

SIGNATURE QUILT No. 1

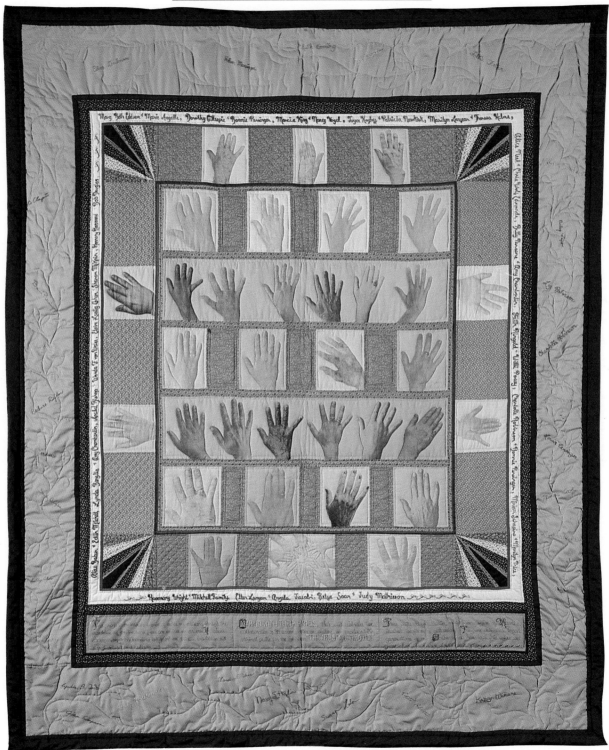

Charlotte Robinson/Quilt Research Staff

1982, Raw silk and cotton, 96″ x 79″

SIGNATURE QUILT NO. 2

Charlotte Robinson/Quilt Research Staff

1983, Raw silk and cotton, 114″ x 90″

QUILT TYPE

Overall pattern up to the surface,
more or less traditional style,
bright flat colors, pieced, and appliqué

ALICE BABER/EDITH MITCHELL
LYNDA BENGLIS/AMY CHAMBERLIN
ELAINE LUSTIG COHEN/SHARON MCKAIN/ROSALIA MEHRINGER
DOROTHY GILLESPIE/BONNIE PERSINGER
JOYCE KOZLOFF/PATRICIA NEWKIRK
BETTY PARSONS/AMY CHAMBERLIN

THE ROAD TO THE CENTER OF THE WORLD

Alice Baber/Edith Mitchell
1980, Cotton and silk, 92″ x 48″

ORIGINAL ARTWORK
THE ROAD TO THE CENTER OF THE WORLD
Alice Baber, 1978, oil on canvas, 90″ x 48″

"Early on, in painting, I had the idea that the place where the forms cross is the important place...the place of transition, or transparency." This oft-heard idea that the site of intersecting elements—trajectories, lines, shapes, colors—is the critical point in a composition, has implications beyond the art of painting.

For a life is circumstantial, the product of intersecting possibilities, and beyond the point of contact (this life, in this time, in this place) extends the indefinite background. Alice Baber made a singular and powerful oeuvre based on the esthetics of crossing transparencies studied most often against a white ground that stands for undifferentiated light.

For many years she exhibited paintings with their floating shapes in ethereal yet saturated hues, shapes that gather momen-tum and are seen to be moving, often, toward an implied distant vortex that might be drawing them "beyond the mountain." Her titles often underline the theme: *The White Bridge to the White Ladder...Open Staircase...Swirls of Sound.* This quilt project was a natural for Baber, who said, "The first thing I loved in painting was being able to get the sheen of silk." When she was a child, a book she prized was called *Fire on the Mountain.* It was about the making of a quilt. She titled her own quilt *The Road to the Center of the World,* and conceived its design as an enlarged version of her usual centripetal image, for "a quilt has its own rules...as: you have to be able to lie under it." In a vivid sense, Alice Baber's own presence shines through this abstract pattern, for she died as the project was nearing fulfillment.

For Baber, as for almost all the artists involved in this project,

Alice Baber and Edith Mitchell selecting fabric for their quilt.

the very making of a quilt implied a connection with time past. In the house of her grandparents and great-grandparents, in central Illinois, there were lots of quilts, many of them signed by ancestors: Lucy, Amos, Callie. These were pioneers who moved westward via the Daniel Boone highway, through Virginia and Kentucky. Her father was a cattleman, farmer, and writer, and her mother made certain Alice had lessons in sewing and embroidery. As a child, she played with marionettes and made their clothes and quilts. Color seems to have called her early. "I'd stand on the front porch of the farmhouse looking out at the fluffy asparagus and say it was *raining green.*"

For Edith Mitchell, the project was also a goad. She collected the original painting, "stuck it on the wall and just went along." Her rendering is an almost literal one, though she was tempted to "go crazy with stitches." Instead, it was—as in Baber's own case—the question of transparencies that became the overriding problem. How to render these intersecting passages, *between* distinct hues, in cloth? (The transparencies in this case are seen on a background of black instead of white.) Not knowing, Mitchell first used transparent textiles, but their own hues turned out to be more intense than anticipated. What is required in cloth is the introduction of a separate patch of in-between shade, to mimic the transition between two intersecting colors. In the end, what took place was clearly a loss of transparency and a re-emphasis on color and textural integrity—the strong interlocked structure—of the painting. A work that in paint may have been "about" evanescence, the

disappearing of colorful clouds into a black vortex, now has been rendered as a work "about" permanence. And Mitchell senses that it might have been done in another way. "I wish I could do it over! I know so much more now."

For Mitchell, it was a "tremendous" opportunity. "Very challenging. I've had only fourteen years of practice after all . . . I'm practically a newcomer. But I'm growing all the time." It was during the Depression that she first learned about quilting, watching her mother sew covers for the family beds when there was no money for blankets. When I asked if any survived as family heirlooms, Mitchell laughed. "We used them till they fell apart." But it is the manual skill and love of the work that has been passed down from mother to daughter and also from her father, who worked as a part-time cabinetmaker.

Being drawn into the far-ranging network of artists in this project was one of its joys for Mitchell, who lives in a small hamlet in the Adirondacks in the workshop/studio/gallery she's operated for some sixteen years: Blue Mountain Designs. It was a pleasure, while she was picking fabrics for the quilt, to travel from place to place with her collection of chips, to fabric stores in "New York, Albany, Saranac Lake, Lake Placid. . . ."

Now Mitchell is back at work as a teacher, lecturer, and professional quilter. She makes commissioned "designer" pieces, quilts in series that just tempt her to "fool with color," and then certain quilts for her own edification and delight. Many of these are of Jack Larsen fabrics, heavy and very colorful. And simple. "I keep telling myself: Keep it simple." ★

Patang

Lynda Benglis/Amy Chamberlin
1980, Cotton, satin, and silk, 94″ x 75″

ORIGINAL ARTWORK
PATANG
Lynda Benglis, 1979, tissue-paper collage, 30" x 22"

Lynda Benglis's vision for this quilt came out of the sky. Came twice out of the sky, one might say, because an early memory of hers is seeing "chemical sunsets" over the oil refineries and chemical plants of the Louisiana coastline where she was born and raised. Benglis came into her perceptual life in a wide, flat land of fantasy cities on the horizon, of broad lakes and soaring bridges. "You fly over it and you can see the Gulf of Mexico and Lake Calcasieu, and two sections of Lake Charles, and a bridge... like a huge flat quilt." Her father was an Orthodox Greek immigrant who worked his way up to prosperity and religious skepticism. Her mother was born in Tennessee, the daughter of a self-made, itinerant Presbyterian minister, who traveled from town to town setting up schools and teaching. "I felt my father was damned to hell. When I was in high school I worried about him, that he'd be damned." Was the need to mediate between the saved and the lost a factor in Benglis's meteoric thrust to

artistic visibility, when she first found herself free of home, liberated, among the feminist revolutionaries of southern California in the early 1970s? To begin with, the California landscape set her free: "space... objects disappearing into the mist ...*huge* distances." It was a long way, studded with flamboyant achievements, to this quilt project into which she has poured her love for "sparkle," and maybe also some feeling of a nearly religious ecstasy. For back there in the 1970s, "my sense of religion transferred immediately to art."

Quilts, homemade by her great-grandmother, were on all the beds in her mother's house. "I'd love to see my clothes go into them." As those old family quilts gathered up patches of the past, so this present quilt gathers, I think, some of the sparkle and gold of the chemical sky. But the immediate inspiration came from India, where not long ago Benglis had a chance to see, during a winter solstice festival, a vision of hundreds of dancing, flashing kites swooping and colliding overhead. The

Quilter Amy Chamberlin with completed Benglis/Chamberlin quilt.

Kite-Day festival is celebrated by villagers who compete in sending up monster fabrications, some of them armed with sharp glass shards knotted into their strings. "You feel you're underwater...so many fish...the sky is full of them, in the trees, on the telephone poles. Such a release!" From that same sight, Benglis took the inspiration for a big tapestry now hanging in the Atlanta, Georgia, International Airport. The bronze mesh forms she is making today, covered with gold leaf for extra gleam, may also carry this double sky-born memory.

Amy Chamberlin, born in central New York, learned her skills making clothes for three daughters. She's a master, especially, of the sewing machine, using it to make portraits and flower-pieces in embroidery. The present quilt provided her with a number of technical challenges. She had not worked before in silks and satins. Benglis bought the silks in India and told her, "Just go wild...and she went wild!" Chamberlin was one of the lucky ones in this respect. Urged to take off on her own, she evolved new design details, embroidering in swirls and S-curves, quilting within the strips, developing concentric rows of quilting stitches in the manner of Hawaiian quilts. "And I thought some dimension would be acceptable, since Benglis is a sculptor, so I used double polyester batting." Each block was made separately and then joined, a row at a time, and finished with a final row of quilting on the joint. It's a splendid achievement. Chamberlin says that just standing in front of it she can feel the vibrations— almost *hear* it.

"I won't hesitate about another project...I won't hesitate to use satins and so on....I love the way light reflects off them." Though she has been a professional working artist since the early 1950s, a teacher, lecturer, and art supervisor in public schools, and has taken first prizes in national quilt shows, the collaboration with Benglis was an expansion—for both of them. The work catches something of the glimmer, shine, and literal elevation of that sky-full of kites. ★

MRS. OLIVER BYRNE'S QUILT

Elaine Lustig Cohen/Sharon McKain/Rosalia Mehringer

1981, Cotton, 70" x 85"

ORIGINAL ARTWORK
MRS. OLIVER BYRNE'S QUILT
Elaine Lustig Cohen, 1980, gouache on paper, 15¾"x 17"

Elaine Lustig Cohen is a strong practitioner of the formalist idiom brought to this country at mid-century by members of the German Bauhaus. At the University of Southern California, where Cohen (then Firstenberg) took her B.F.A. in the late 1940s, she studied painting, and later met and married designer Alvin Lustig. For seven years, she worked in his office, specializing in graphic design, later moving back to New York. After Lustig's death she did freelance designing, gradually moving into other fields. She's an expert technician, a master of materials, with a bold sense of pattern. She has worked in the flat and in the round, in painting, print-making, and sculpture, and is now joining modes in large painted boxes. The wood surface is gessoed and a stark geometric pattern laid down with tapes and pencil lines. What's fun, she says, is to figure it out. This drive to put things together, to join craft to art, color to shape, wood to canvas to cloth, is her way of exercising a family gift. Her father was a plumbing contractor, a man who worked with his hands and made things connect and *work*. Her mother encouraged her to *become* something: that poignant encouragement from one without opportunity to do so herself that is so often heard in the life stories of younger women artists. Her mother, a year before she died, took up needlepoint, copied one of Cohen's paintings, and asked, "Can I put my initials next to yours?"

Cohen owns a number of quilts, among them a handsome Shaker piece, and has a couple hanging on the wall. But her delight in the quilt project was, it seems, principally a *working*, non-theoretical one: "A great opportunity to work in another medium. I love that idea. It pushed me in another direction." The process appealed to her as a different mode of collage, an unexpected and otherwise difficult-to-come-by combination of hard geometric patterning and soft material. (There are, in other words, two opposing attractions in quiltmaking, or can be: to be neat, and to enjoy the scrappiness of the cloth-pile.) For her design, she turned to a treasure of a book she had just discovered at a New York book fair. It was a nineteenth-century rendering of the first six books of Euclid by means of geometric illustrations in color. The author and inventor of this imaginative work was one Oliver Byrne (which is why the quilt is titled *Mrs. Oliver Byrne's Quilt*). It was the author's idea that women, being especially sensitive to colors, would benefit by his treatment of the abstract principles:

We are happy to find that the elements of mathematics now form a considerable part of every sound female education. Therefore we call the attention of those interested or engaged in the education of ladies to this very attractive mode of communicating knowledge.

Sharon McKain's grandmother taught her to sew by hand and on the machine; that grandmother could simply put her hands together, holding two bobbins, and in a flash turn out beautiful

Sharon McKain and Elaine Lustig Cohen studying design for their quilt.

lace. Patiently, apparently doting on her granddaughter, she taught McKain to sew and in general to be comfortable with needle and thread. Afternoons and weekends, the women in the family would work together.

Later, when she was married, McKain made her first quilt. It took almost a year and by that time she had had her first child, so it was time for a crib quilt. Little by little in this way she taught herself the basics. When she moved with her husband to the small fishing village of Noank, Connecticut, a women she met at a church bazaar taught her the more complicated steps. And "the more you work with fabric, the more you learn."

One of the things both artists had to learn by doing was how colors change character and weight when they are transposed into cloth and enlarged. The first trial run was all wrong. The forms were too big. There is a size in quilting, McKain explains, anything beyond about eight by ten inches, where a color-patch becomes too big, too distracting. And even the colors themselves—red, white, and blue—looked like a flag when they were blown up.

One day Cohen traveled to McKain's studio and the two of them sat around trying to decide how to handle the problem. Eventually they cut down the scale of the repeat pattern, took out blue altogether, brought up the maroon. Then they worked from a lifesize mockup, step by step. "It was fun to work together, like a couple of old friends," says the quilter.

The after-effects have worked both ways. McKain has gone back to school and become a photographer. "Suddenly she realized she wasn't a quiltmaker at all...she was an artist," says Cohen.

For Cohen, "The best of it was the collaboration." ★

UNTITLED

Dorothy Gillespie/Bonnie Persinger

1982, Cotton, 108″ x 45″

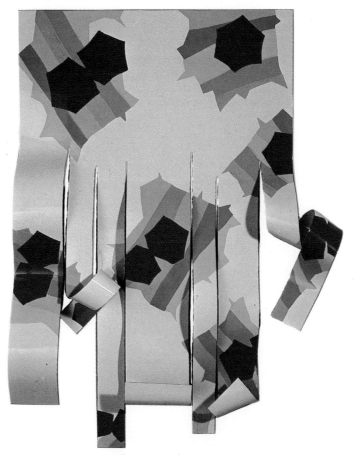

ORIGINAL ARTWORK
ARRANGEMENT TO THE SOUND OF A FLUTE
Dorothy Gillespie, 1980, painted metal sculpture, 46″ x 34″ x 8″

"I build bridges," says Dorothy Gillespie. "I can go back and do anything I've done before. I can do blocks . . . all kinds of things." Those "blocks" are small constructions she made at one point, like the building blocks of children. Gillespie has also worked in metals, Mylar, plastics, porcelain, canvas, paper, and cloth. She's developed three-dimensional abstract canvas structures one can enter, large standing cylinders of painted cardboard, constructs of large rolls of paper, some of them fifty feet long. Her latest works are wall pieces, metal ribbons painted in brilliant colors that lap and twist out from the flat surface. Her solution to the quilt project was a work that hangs straight down the wall and rolls onto the floor in a soft curve that would, theoretically, be the bolster for a bed. Her quilter, Bonnie Persinger, likes the fact that it "comes off the wall." She finds the design "bouncy." It's big, very bold, very energetic. Blue angular shapes come pell-mell as if plowing down the white path of the ground, to collide upon the floor. Persinger herself has made very large soft-sculpture quilts in recent years.

In 1976 for example, she made a *Corn Quilt*, like a giant ear of corn, that was exhibited around the country in that bicentennial year. "It's six feet tall, body size! You can barely get your arms around it. I was trying to blend quilts and soft sculpture."

The collaboration was clearly successful partly because these two artists' sense of scale, of "body size" presence, were akin, and partly perhaps because of a geographical bond between them: both grew up in the South. Gillespie's memory of childhood seems to reverberate throughout her work. Her father was a construction engineer for Standard Oil in Roanoke, Virginia. He made machinery for the oil pumps, but he could not draw, so Dorothy did the drawings for him. In fact, her father made her his special sidekick. Every evening they went together down to the local railroad station to put the mail on the train to Richmond. Every night, father and daughter stood by the tracks watching the headlight of the locomotive appear out of the dark, coming toward them down the tracks. Could it be that the linear character of Gillespie's mature work, notably this quilt, rolling

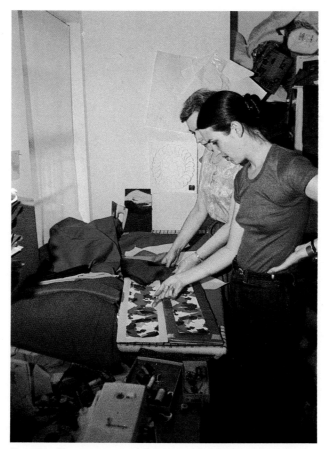

Bonnie Persinger consulting with Amy Chamberlin about choice of fabric for Gillespie/Persinger quilt.

down the wall to strike the floor and curl upward—that rush of glowing shapes kept to a narrow roadbed—captures a memory of those evenings watching for the train? And in New York, Gillespie gets up at dawn every morning to be in her studio by 6:15 a.m. so she can roll her metal sculptures in the metalpress.

Quilting and needlework were regular tasks in Gillespie's family. Her mother was an excellent seamstress and Gillespie herself, at eleven, made a small *Yo-Yo* quilt. At home the hanging and changing of fabrics marked the seasons. Curtains, rugs, and slipcovers were changed in spring and fall: light textures and colors in the spring; dark ones in the autumn. It was a big job, a ritual: unpacking, brushing, mending, hanging, and folding.

Persinger has a theory that the activity of sewing skips generations. Her own grandmother—like the grandmother of almost every artist represented here—sewed, while her mother did not. Again, as often seems the case, it was the father who was a craftsperson, in this case a jeweler. But both parents encouraged her to make all kinds of things, dolls and doll clothes, stuffed animals, and so forth. Eventually, when she began to grow herself, eventually pushing up to close to six feet, like Wenda von Weise who lived with the same challenge, she had to make all her own clothes. "I don't remember ever *not* making things!"

Gillespie's quilt design came to its fabricator as a painting. Persinger picked the fabrics and sewed the top. They met to discuss the stitching, and then Persinger quilted it. Both these artists were among the original instigators of the project back in 1976, when a group began to talk about making a bicentennial quilt. Persinger has moved on to other projects since then. Her studio is in her house; there she stores her "tons of fabrics," her shelves of thread, her sewing machine. Having "exploded" out of that one room, she has set up her quilting frame in the living room. She teaches and organizes quilt shows. She also designs printed circuit-boards for a computer firm, doing the intricate, time-consuming laying out of the board on which the memory chips are mounted, work that is both fascinating and dull, demanding exactitude and patience—very like quilting. ★

UNTITLED

Joyce Kozloff/Patricia Newkirk

1981, Cotton, 101″ x 73″

ORIGINAL ARTWORK
STUDY FOR A PATCHWORK QUILT
Joyce Kozloff, 1976, color pencil on paper, 40″ x 30″

"I don't know where she would have found another quiltma-ker with an *engineering* approach to the work," said Patricia Newkirk. Born in Ashland, Kentucky, Newkirk is the daughter of an electrician; as a child she harbored the then-unrealizable dream of becoming an engineer. She liked putting things together, hand-detail, perfection of crafts-manship. She learned quilting from her grandmother—learned to piece the tops, that is, but not to do the actual quilting until a moment some years ago when she realized the time had come: "Grandma wasn't always going to be around; I'd better learn. So on New Year's Day we put a top in the frame..." Since then she's become an expert, a teacher of the art, a member of the Board of Directors and twice President of the National Quilt Association, and a widely published writer on quiltmaking. She found this project "just fine." Joyce Kozloff provided a strong, geometric pattern that, moreover, pushed Newkirk into a new field: color. "The best thing I learned was that I could handle color. I'd always used monochromatic earth tones. I never felt I had creativity with colors. This was such a challenge! I learned a lot about *me*: maybe I *am* an artist!"

The artists went together to fabric houses, took immense baskets of remnants, dumped them on the floor and sorted. "I chose," says Kozloff, "she matched...or she chose and never made a mistake." Eventually nearly a hundred different fabrics were introduced into the quilt, some of nearly imperceptible segues between tones. Kozloff had been able to provide only a poor slide of a drawing done in 1976 and then sold. Newkirk had it enlarged; she studied it and realized there were really two designs here: one in the center, one around the borders. Eventu-ally, she sewed the center as a single unit, and the border as a unit, then joined them. In addition, the corners had to be restudied; in the end they were designed as small variations on the star-pattern in the central block. The whole process was time-consuming: Close to two thousand hours of the quilter's labor went into it and "believe me, that's a lot; there's no way to be repaid for that kind of time." But making this complex and challenging work pushed Newkirk along in a direction she was already headed. Back in 1960, she had applied to the Maryland School of Engineering, but her admission application was refused. Since beginning this quilt in 1976, she has earned a

Joyce Kozloff describes Kozloff/Newkirk quilt for a PBS film crew.

B.A. in economics and nearly finished her M.A. in labor studies. "Perfecting the art," as a way of life, can apply to many kinds of work.

Kozloff's instinct for design impelled this cooperative project forward. Her own development as an artist has taken her through stages of exploration and refinement, and her coming of age, artistically, at the time of the Women's Movement with its liberating openness to pattern art rooted in the anonymous handcrafts gave her the invitation she needed. And for a printmaking session at June Wayne's Tamarind Workshop, where she began to invent new textures and patterns, "I'll be forever grateful. The work became more graphic, richer, and this led to the next group of patterns."

The grid, the wall: these confining yet challenging concepts underlie much of Kozloff's work and language. She grew up in New Jersey, in "a small gridded place," a contained neighborhood of working-class people, almost all of whom were employed, at one time or another, at the local Johns Mansfield factory. That building, its dark brick smokestacks, its gray walls, lay on everybody's horizon, or just beyond the square-edge of the block. "I don't like to think about it." The trouble was asbestos. "The stuff dropped from the sky. Everyone knew what it was. People had lung disease." Across the small domestic grid of lawns, sidewalks, streets, this malevolent air blew at will.

Later, when Kozloff was living in California, she experienced a season of brush fires of the kind that threaten lives and real estate up and down the coast. "You could see the hot, dry, billowing smoke, the huge fires."

There was another memory, too, that may have surfaced in Kozloff's first paintings, where dark smoky tones predominate. In 1968 she visited Sicily, arriving at Agrigento at sunset. "It was dusk. There was a dark feeling associated with the place. Temples with columns...the complex of temples, seeing through one to another." Her quilt pattern with its turning stars in squares makes reference to various traditions: some vestige of a classical mosaic, Islamic tiles, the quilt patterns of old. Isn't it a magic instrument: a gridded wall to contain and keep out smoke that is allowed to break forth only in brilliant colors? ★

UNTITLED

Betty Parsons/Amy Chamberlin

1980, Cotton, velveteen, and corduroy, 71″ x 96″

ORIGINAL ARTWORK
VILLAGE SHOP
Betty Parsons, 1980, wood and paint sculpture, 18″ x 12½″ x 4″

Betty Parsons describing Parsons/Chamberlin quilt.

Betty Parsons, who died in July 1982, was a sophisticated woman, and her quilt has the frontal, jouncing, even gawky directness of a master practitioner's foray into an unexpected medium. I see the image as a turning star, a primitivistic variant on the great star motif that adorned the most splendid traditional quilts. Here, too, repeated circles introduce elements of "sky" and "moon." The design contains ample amounts of those ingredients Mies van der Rohe said were foremost in a work of art or an art-making person—clarity and energy—and that Parsons once said were fundamental to her own life.

Her New York gallery was a famous center for the art world from the mid-1940s; there she showed the major figures of the Abstract Expressionist movement before and until their ascent to economic success. As an artist-connoisseur, she was awakened to abstract art at the 1913 Armory Show in New York. Later she worked with sculptor Alexander Archipenko; in 1947 she began painting on her own. Still, like many women of her age, it wasn't until the feminist-powered 1960s and 1970s that she really put her own work forward. Sophisticated she may have been, but her art had a childlike quality. It was, in fact, by painting beach stones, in 1966, that she began to liberate her hand and use bright colors. Painter Jack Youngerman urged her to do so, and later a trip to Africa pushed her further in that direction. "I had a sense of *life*," she said of herself. "Anything that diminished my feeling of life, that crushed me, I hated. I had a fantastic feeling for... life."

Amy Chamberlin was, she confesses, awed by Parson's reputation. Working from an original twelve-by-fifteen-inch painting blown up in a slide projector, she gathered the fabrics, completed the top, and then carried it to New York, to the famous gallery on 57th Street. She had struggled with some areas. The blue circles she had rendered in velveteen, "because Parsons struck me as a sophisticated lady. But when I walked into the gallery, there she was in blue jeans and a gingham shirt." It was logical then to switch fabrics, to substitute denim and corduroy, and "the blue jean texture resolved the problem."

Silks and satins, stripes and flying kites in the Benglis collaboration... denim and corduroy in the collaboration with Parsons: in each case, the material itself provided the key to the successful rendering of the idea into cloth. The transfer was an inventive one most often achieved by artist and quilter working together. No mere duplication of an idea, it was a genuine reformulation of the design. ★

QUILT TYPE

Figurative or symbolic dominant image,
frontal and enlarged, appliqué

MARY BETH EDELSON/MARIE GRIFFIN INGALLS
HARMONY HAMMOND/BOB DOUGLAS
ALICE NEEL/CHRIS WOLF EDMONDS

WOMEN RISING

Mary Beth Edelson/Marie Griffin Ingalls

1977, Cotton, 85" x 85"

ORIGINAL ARTWORK
SLEEP IN THE ARMS OF THE GREAT MOTHER
Mary Beth Edelson, 1975, mixed media on jute tag paper, 24″ x 30″

"I, too, like to create," says Marie Griffin Ingalls, voicing a complaint heard from a small number of the quilters in this project who felt some frustration rendering another artist's design in cloth. Understandably, the collaboration worked best when an image could be recast for the cloth medium, when the cloth-artist had as much innovative exploratory work to do as the designer.

Ingalls is herself a specialist, in crewel and embroidery, and only occasionally makes a quilt. But in this case, the problem was quite specifically to enlarge a small scheme and then to make the required adjustments of scale and detail. For example, certain passages of lettered text could not be rendered in cloth. As she worked, Ingalls came to appreciate the scope of Mary Beth Edelson's design, and took pleasure in doing the appliqué. In the end, she had incorporated many kinds of stitchery: "appliqué and crewel, and crewel yarn and embroidery floss . . . and quilting in small hand-stitches."

Ingalls comes from a family of needleworkers. She cherishes an heirloom piece of dyed wool stuffed-work made by her great-grandmother. Her grandmother, too, was an expert, specializing in handsewn and crochetted trousseaux for brides—camisoles and yoked undergarments. Ingalls herself, who lives both in Washington, D.C., and in a big house on the Pungo River in Virginia, has inherited the gift: She makes cloth dolls with trousseaux of clothes that are sold commercially. So have her twin daughters, who make their own dolls, and so, in his way, has her son, a mountain climber/mathematician/photographer.

Mary Beth Edelson surrounded by her drawings for Edelson/Ingalls quilt.

For Edelson, the quilt image had its origin some years ago when she took part in a Jungian discussion group and began working with the figure of the Great Goddess. By the late 1970s, that image had become central to feminist theory, and Edelson adapted it in many ways. She created happenings at outdoor and indoor sites, making use of fire, water, smoke, and stone. She developed rituals to be enacted by groups of women, and made conceptual book projects. When the quilt program came along in the late 1970s, Edelson contributed a small painting for transfer into cloth. As it turned out, she did much of the scaling herself, and eventually pinned into place the pieces to be appliquéd.

She has since moved on to other themes. She has begun a series of acrylic paintings on the folklore character of the "Trickster Rabbit," a loping fellow with long ears, symbol of rampant energy, a personage half wicked, half divine. These works may have been influenced somewhat by the quilt project, for the canvas ground is ironed to hold its irregular shape on the wall, a little like a hung-up bedcover. But Edelson's work is highly politicized; deliberately exploiting the expressionist mode of some male artists these days, she has set herself the mission of opposing their "death-oriented" imagery. She is a force for an expanding militant feminist consciousness that craves connection with a universal language. And is this two-pronged search not analogous to the quilt—that union of idiosyncratic surface elaboration with a ground of heavy padded cloth?

Yet some viewers may feel there is an esthetic problem with Edelson's quilt as it stands. The image of the Goddess, so central to the artist's consciousness, may remain a motif imprinted on the ground, not risen *materially* out of it. "This life-force, that's what I feel in this Goddess, emerging from the earth," says Edelson, most movingly. But is that so in the sense of the symbolic "earth" at hand—that is, the cloth itself? Purists of the quilt idiom may find cause for discussion here. The work may impress us as more of a banner than a quilt, an insignia or icon to be displayed on a wall or as a standard. Thus we learn as well from works that deviate, however strikingly, from the presented norm in this project. ★

FAN LADY MEETS RUFFLED WATERS

Harmony Hammond/Bob Douglas

1983, Cotton, 75″ x 90″

ORIGINAL ARTWORK
FAN LADY MEETS RUFFLED WATERS
Harmony Hammond, 1982, acrylic and oil crayon on paper, 30″ x 40″

Harmony Hammond has evolved two distinct manners of working in a career that has won her considerable attention. On the one hand, she has made and shown very large wrapped cloth "presences" that lean against the wall or hang on it, touching, seeming to embrace or hug or reach out in humanoid gestures. These ample creatures project humanist feelings as well. They are tender or awkward or—as in her latest work—frightening. That very large figure is called *Kudzu*, after the weed that grows rampant in the South, devouring landscape in its voracious expansion. The work is black and bifurcated down the middle, like ribs, or clutching hands. It, and the other personages in Hammond's atelier, begs to be acknowledged, to be argued with or comforted. On the other hand, she has invented a set of engaging Klee-like figures, "Fan Lady," "Ruffled Waters" and others, who dally and prance back and forth across flat painted canvases.[1] It's this two-dimensional idiom that Hammond adapted for her quilt design. She provided the quilter, Bob Douglas, with a small painting and a full-size tissue rendering. The women shopped for fabric together. Douglas did the cloth

blowup, adjusted the scale of the figures, and went to work on the sewn details: braided edges and a richly stitched ground behind the figures. She had, along the way, worked on several other quilts, including the *Signature*, but this was her first chance to do one from the outset, and she was enthusiastic.

As it transpired, however, the "artist" here was also a trained cloth-worker, and, if a distinction were to be made between the categories of designer and renderer, she might be said to have invaded her colleague's territory. For it was Hammond who determined the kind of quilting pattern to be laid down on both the front and back of the work. Such jockeying for leadership was inevitable, for Hammond had studied fashion illustration and dress design at the Art Institute of Chicago. She came into consciousness as an artist in that environment of students in black leotards and turtlenecks, of paint-speckled floors and smocks, of nude models and feminist work-circles. It was her spirit-opening period, when she was young and looking for a way out of hometown conventionality. The fans and ruffles, "spirit dots," and general air of ebullient cockiness in her clothlike painted figures must all arise out of that period.

Harmony Hammond (right) explaining details from her quilt design to Bob Douglas.

Both women come from sewing ancestors. Hammond's grandmother was an expert seamstress and turned out Christmas dresses, complete with pinafores and ruffles, for the children. Douglas's grandmother was a fancy milliner in New York, and her skill and industry were reborn in Douglas. "I have her thimble. I love wearing her thimble. Whatever enabled her, did me too." Still, when she made her first quilt, it was "a disaster. We gave it to the dog. The dog rejected it. The second was passable, and every one since then has been a commissioned work." Now she runs a store and quilts when she has time. Time is of the essence for both women. Both have children: Hammond, a daughter, Douglas, twin sons, all teenagers. Hammond goes so far as to attribute the very shape of her sculptural work to her life as a mother. "Wrapping with cloth you can work in fragmented time. I can wrap for two hours, then deal with Tanya, and if I don't come back for two days it's not the end of the world. I use every scrap of time. If I waited till I had four hours, I'd never have made what I did."

Both women loved the deep saturated purple cloth they chose for the background of this quilt. For Douglas, it was an inspira-tion. "It has become almost a tapestry, heavily textured with raised sections that cast shadows. I love the softness, the depth." And she has lavished invention on the details. "I added padding to raise the border as if it were a frame. But then I got caught up in the purple, and decided I didn't like the distraction." For the spiral-body of the "Fan Lady," she envisioned a mola technique: cutting through a top layer of cloth to reveal a contrasting color.

The design "works" in a perfectly suitable way, yet one might feel that this collaboration, begun late in the project, could have used more time. What strange expansions of the "quilt" might have taken place had Hammond decided, as certain others here did, to take on the more difficult task of translating a sculptural concept into flat cloth? Such a program might have challenged both women to explore the "meaning" of such a work as *Kudzu*, with its undeniable sexual overtones, and to reformulate that meaning in the language of historical bed-art. Perhaps this is a project for the future. ★

NOTE

1. Along the way she also showed a number of floor-pieces that were braided and painted "rugs".

OLIVIA IN BLUE HAT

Alice Neel/Chris Wolf Edmonds
1981, Cotton, 75" x 43"

ORIGINAL ARTWORK
OLIVIA IN BLUE HAT
Alice Neel, 1973, oil on canvas, 45″ x 22″

"At the Met in the old days, I'd go see quilts and think, 'What great abstractions!'" So, contrary rebel that she is, Alice Neel determined, when she agreed to do a quilt design, to make it figurative. It is well known that she developed her coruscating realist-expressionist line when she turned to drawing during a time of mental breakdown years ago. Concentration on the person she was drawing was to be a means to the reconstruction of her mind. I find it interesting that for this project she chose not one of the "freakish" images in her vocabulary, however, but one of her tender works, a portrait of her granddaughter, *Olivia in Blue Hat*, done in 1973. And the transposition of the image to cloth led to interesting changes. Rendered in the large blocks required to build up flesh areas, Neel's pattern here cannot be said to be a linear one. Her famous line fades out of importance, overwhelmed by color. It functions less as outline than as mere border between color areas. It is de-energized, and the work assumes an aspect quite uncharacteristic of this artist. Anxiety, pain, anguish—qualities Neel is expert in rendering—are absent from this work. Instead, the power of her constructive intelligence is revealed. That dark blue hat, the flat white undergarment, the shadows: these stand, in cloth, as stark structural blocks in a composition that might be called Neel "stripped bare."

Chris Wolf Edmonds and Alice Neel deciding on the quilting design for
Olivia in Blue Hat *at Neel's studio in 1978.*

Chris Wolf Edmonds found the project a challenge. As a painter, "Neel can blend colors. I learned a lot about skin tones. I'd done quilts before with a figure on a field, but never with so much skin exposed. I found it most difficult! I realized there were hues my logical mind hadn't told me were in skin. After making this quilt, I've begun dyeing my own cloth to achieve various values of one color for my geometric quilts."

Edmonds progressed from needlecraft hobbyist trying "to make something pretty to decorate the house," to the place where most of the quilters in this project stand today: "trying to develop quilting as a serious art form." She is self-taught, although her family did needlework and a grandmother quilted. Still, it was not until the new wave of interest in the idiom that she found herself really involved, around 1965.

Now she is engaged with all the steps in the making of a quilt: designing, cutting, marking. She executes commissions for individuals and organizations, and has made a quilt-wall-hanging, celebrating pioneer women, for the City Hall of Lawrence, Kansas. She also teaches and lectures throughout the country. Expertise generates its own momentum: "The more you do, the more you enjoy and the more you invent." Now she is making geometric works with color values manipulated to suggest dimensionality or transparency. For these, she makes no color mockup but lets the colors take their shapes and places as she works with the fabrics: a most "painterly" way to operate; "spontaneous" is the word she uses. ★

Alice Neel, being interviewed by Penny McMorris for PBS film, in Robinson's studio in 1981.

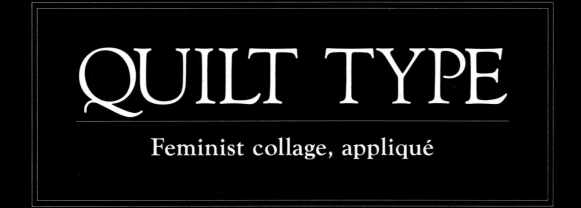

QUILT TYPE

Feminist collage, appliqué

ELLEN LANYON/ANGELA JACOBI

BETYE SAAR/JUDY MATHIESON

MIRIAM SCHAPIRO/MARILYN PRICE

ROSEMARY WRIGHT/THE MITCHELL FAMILY/BOB DOUGLAS

STARWORT PHENOMENA

Ellen Lanyon/Angela Jacobi

1981, Cotton and silk, 93″ x 69″

ORIGINAL ARTWORK
STARWORT PHENOMENA,
Ellen Lanyon, 1981, watercolor and ink on paper, 11″ x 8½″

Chicagoan Ellen Lanyon has exhibited her vivid realistic/surrealistic work since the mid 1940s. Winner of numerous awards, she is equally well known in New York and in the Midwest. During the feminist turmoil of the 1970s, Lanyon emerged as one of the most articulate spokeswomen of the new ideas.

As she explains it, her present idiom took shape late in that decade when she was commissioned by the Container Corporation of America to make one in their famous series of ads by fine artists. Her theme was a statement by Edith Wharton on Renaissance anatomist Vesalius. To show the successive layers of flesh, muscle, and bone in the human body, Vesalius drew an upright figure in a lifelike pose, but then "peeled back" layers—revealing the hidden anatomy.

This illustrative technique was a revelation to Lanyon, who had been looking for a way of showing the insides of her subjects. "I'd been dealing with the theme of magic, stage magic ...the idea of illusion. I thought of my paintings as screens, steps in a magic presentation." Her adaptation of the device uses a painted hand that acts as magician, as though it were "tearing off the page."

In her design *Starwort Phenomena,* Lanyon reverses the device. Here a surface "painting" of flowers on a black ground is "peeled back" to reveal an occult hand holding folded papers, one of which is marked with a star. Lanyon's image is directly related to childhood experience: Cousins and uncles ran funeral parlors. As a child she played alongside coffins, stood around the embalming room, and watched bodies being readied with waxes and powders. Sitting on a casket, she puffed at her first cigarette, thinking quite clearly, "If mother knew, she'd die."

But "mother" was a Christian Scientist, for whom "death" had no doctrinal reality. Would it be forcing an issue to suggest that between these two antithetical views of death—that it has no dominion, and that it is the basic stuff of a workingman's work—artist Lanyon conceived thoughts, and eventually images, that found their authentic expression in the curious images of her art?

The quilter in this collaboration was an old friend of Lanyon's, whom she considers an artist in stitchery. Angela Jacobi is of Greek origin; her family included many needleworkers and embroiderers—experts in all the handicrafts, including weaving. Jacobi sets high standards and expectations for herself, and the

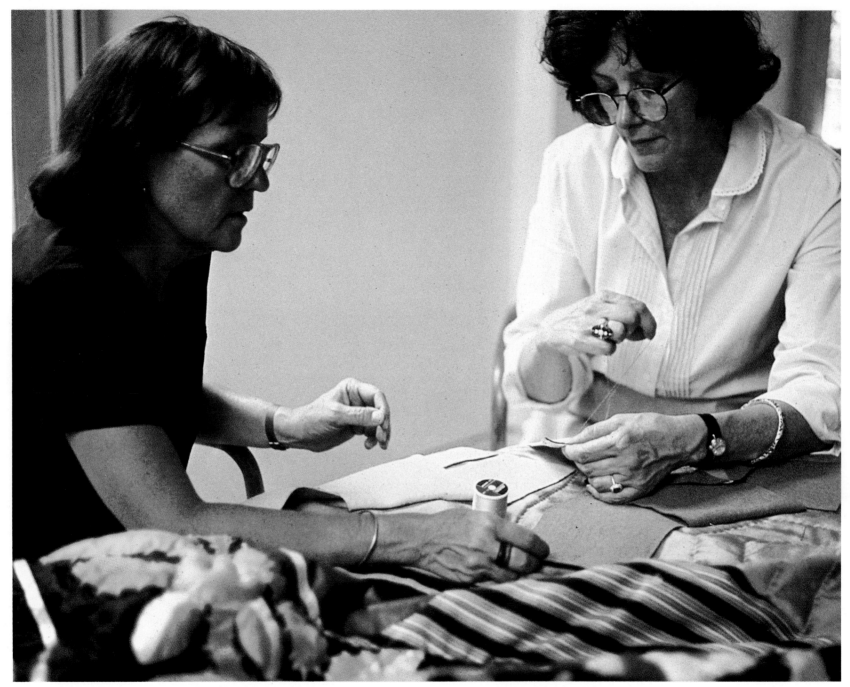

Ellen Lanyon and Angela Jacobi test fabric samples for their quilt.

challenges of transposing the difficult design for *Starwort Phenomena* are another story. This is a quilt stitched entirely by hand, worked on for long hours against a deadline, using materials to which Jacobi developed an allergy.

Starwort Phenomena is "a smashing design with great potential." The design, and the problems the artists confronted, raise basic questions about the issue of transposition of an image from medium to medium. Would there have been a more "material," less illustrative, way to suggest "peeling back," "revealing underneath layers" in the medium of *quilt*, which is, by its very nature, a structure of layers? Such questions are among the interesting by-products of this collaborative endeavor. ★

FANTASIES

Betye Saar/Judy Mathieson

1981, Cotton, 86″ x 61″

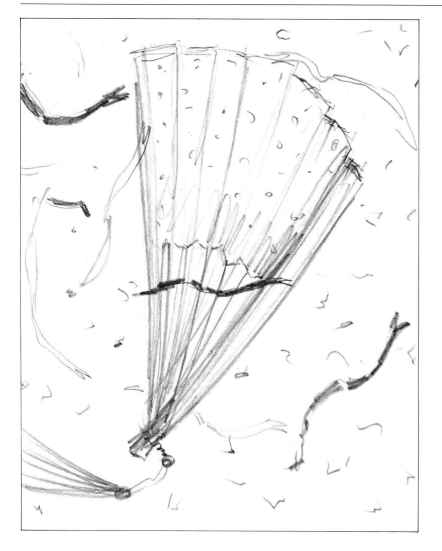

ORIGINAL ARTWORK
FANS AND HEARTS
Betye Saar, 1981, pencil on paper, 11″ x 8½″

Betye Saar and Judy Mathieson, friends and near neighbors in southern California, worked in close collaboration. In the end, this very closeness exposed differences in their working methods and, perhaps more fundamentally, in their styles. All the same, the viewer may feel that the charm and delicacy and, somehow, the appropriateness of the design to the medium, reflect a happy mutuality of inspiration. The reason may be because Saar is used to working in collage and is much embroiled in her collection of "things"—cloth, wood, paper, images of all kinds from dolls to fans, including all the drift of objects that come through a household.

Growing up in the Watts area of Los Angeles, she was a born picker and saver of bits of things. She has designed costumes and worked in many media, from color Xerox to rattan and raffia.

The mothers of both these women sewed; Saar's was a professional seamstress after her husband, a literary and philosophical man, died. Mathieson's mother made her family's clothing. She herself has taken instruction in batik, tie-dye, and other cloth techniques and was "converted" to quilting only a few years ago. It was perhaps as much the community of quiltmakers that appealed to her, as it was, she explains, that power a quiltmaker has to make "art" out of scraps.

The women sorted through Saar's collection, and decided to use handkerchiefs and fans. Mathieson adapted the fan idea and constructed about ten samples in mockup. Together they shopped for fabrics, though in the end it was Mathieson who

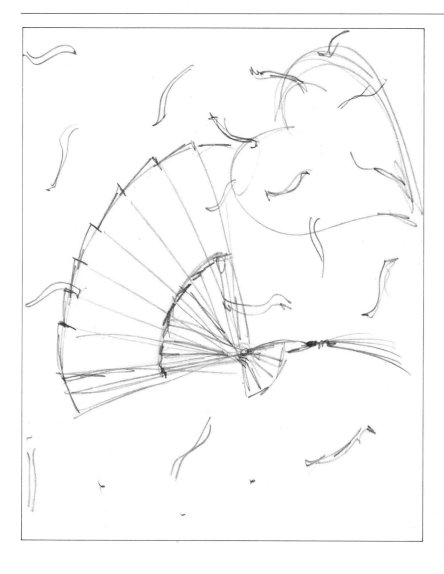

Betye Saar sketching fans and hearts for her quilt.

made the final choices. Then, meeting at Mathieson's studio, the two began to pin the fans into place—a long process.

Saar, the "artist," was open to whim in placing the objects. When it became evident that more shapes were needed, she added some hearts. Mathieson added some handkerchiefs. Saar, working as she usually does, moved the shapes around by feel or look, trying for a composition with a sense of randomness, as if the elements were floating. Mathieson, however, is used to a more controlled, pre-planned way of working. She plots her quilts on a grid, uses straight lines, works them out on graph paper. Lately she has even been making quilts based on the look of those little puzzles made of interlocking pieces of wood. Working by intuition was new for her, and it led her to question the essential differences between "artist" and "craftsperson."

"Artists call their work 'a piece,'" she says. "I prefer 'cup,' or 'saucer'. I like, 'that's a skirt. That's a quilt.'"

"What the 'artist' does is 'art.' What I do is 'work.' A person spends a thousand hours embroidering someone else's design. Yet in the end, it's 'her [the designer's] piece.' It's as if the artist were on one floor and the quiltmaker on another, and the stair is blocked. Now that the project is over, I feel better. I won't work again on someone else's design. My way of working didn't rub off on her, and her way is very different. She was very responsive, yet in the end, I felt it was her design."

This friendly jostling could not have been avoided in a collaborative project pairing off individuals with strong tastes; the liveliness—and appropriateness—of the design is a credit to their mutual sensitivity. ★

THE PHOENIX HEART

Miriam Schapiro/Marilyn Price

1981, Hand silk-screened cotton, 82″ x 82″

ORIGINAL ARTWORK
HEART
Miriam Schapiro, 1981, acrylic and fabric on canvas, 63″ x 69″

This was one of the strongest, happiest collaborations, perhaps because the artists could meet several times, first in Kalamazoo, Michigan, while Miriam Schapiro's traveling retrospective was on view there, then in New York and Long Island. Schapiro modified her quilt design on the basis of technical advice from Marilyn Price, who developed a special silk-screening process for it.

Both these artists share an enthusiasm for feminist projects. To make the quilt, Price set up a small cooperative enterprise, hiring five women to do the hand-quilting at the local Arts Center, with a grant from the Michigan State Arts Commission.[1] In return, Price offered the public a week-long workshop in silk-screening. Some six hundred hours of drudgery were provided for, with a minimum of pain—Schapiro calls this solution "spicy."

The design, like all the work of this strong, formally oriented and politically concerned artist, straddles eras and definitions. It presents a heart, boldly centered on a black ground—an image at once sentimental, historical, and visually striking. Moreover, the heart is silk-screened in the old "babyblock" quilt pattern. "I've been working with the babyblock idea for years," says Schapiro; during her excursions into hard-edge forms in the 1960s, she made a number of works that involved similar geometric patterns. Price prepared a number of samples showing

Marilyn Price machine-appliquéing a portion of The Phoenix Heart.

the pattern screened in transparent dyes of various intensities on patterned fabrics. Schapiro made her choice and cut out the fabric flowers; then Price appliquéd them on. In sum, the image is a layered one, built up from the black ground step by step, as historical records might be said to accumulate level by level. "I wanted a heart," says Schapiro. "Over and over the heart appears in traditional quilts. I wanted the heart as an icon. And I wanted black, because in quilts, it's rare." Thus a dialectic between the geometric and the iconic, between hard and soft, curve and square-edge, impersonal and emotional, proceeded as it does throughout the course of Schapiro's career.

Both artists in this collaboration claim to have grown by virtue of it. Schapiro has moved on to very large works. One new painting, *Invitation*, looks at first like a huge painted quilt, but

reveals itself as the diagram of an elaborately laid table. The grid of the babyblock may have led, in turn, to a smaller work, *Autobiography*, which presents seventy small images in rows like votive figures, spelling out the artist's life story. The collection is random but meaningful, and includes a number of religious symbols—menorah, cross, and star.

Schapiro's quest is here, as it has long been, for a communicative art. "We were overwhelmed by the mysticism of the 1950s. Now I think art should speak with greater clarity, more relevance."

For her part, Price found working with Schapiro "helped me sharpen my own images." As most of the quilters did, she had learned sewing skills from her mother, a dressmaker; but she then spent some twenty years as a printmaker before coming

Art historians Mary Garrard and Norma Broude admire quilt by Schapiro/ Price.

back to fabrics in the early 1970s. She takes joy in the potential for freedom of scale of the found-again medium of cloth. "On paper you can't go much over about three feet. But with fabrics you can go to any size. New worlds opened to me." Freed by working on cloth, Price found that her audience, too, had expanded. Now she is doing large commissioned works for public buildings, in a combination of screen and quilting, that focus on figurative images that speak to her public at large.

Here is a concept working itself into consciousness through the material language of cloth, thread, and imagery: a sense of a larger power breaking out of the power exercised over traditional materials at hand. "I had tremendous respect for Price," says Schapiro. "She is so secure; her technical knowledge so advanced. It couldn't have been done without her." ★

Note

1. The assisting quilters were Carol Clemons, Virginia Koehler, Mary Kay Horn, Beryl Poland and Janet Robertson.

THE MITCHELL FAMILY QUILT

Rosemary Wright/The Mitchell Family/Bob Douglas

1983, Cotton, 88″ x 84″

ORIGINAL ARTWORK
WORKING DRAWING
Rosemary Wright, 1982, mixed media on paper, 30″ x 30″

The quilt designed by Rosemary Wright, like the one designed by Marilyn Lanfear, literally reaches out into extended, separated families and symbolically reunites them. Wright was born into an Irish Catholic farming community in Indiana. Her people were "great problem solvers... creative on a basic level." Her grandmother and aunt made quilts; her mother designed clothes, and in the 1950s wrote a seminal book on innovative leatherworking. But after remarriage, Wright's mother moved the family to another part of the country and another "class," and the ties to place and people were broken for a while. Wright took a degree in sculpture and aesthetics, then spent two years in Asia studying pottery.

Meanwhile, she began to investigate Jungian ideas and concluded that the theory of archetypes was applicable to her own work, mixed-media conceptual exhibitions she presented for galleries in New York and Washington, D.C. Moving back and forth between making and theory, Wright lectures and teaches, and has held artist-in-residence posts. When she was asked to join in the quilt project, "I said no at first. I had no wish to make a quilt. But just about then my marriage broke up, and I began thinking about the parts of my family I'd been cut off from for twenty years. I realized what I was thinking about was *not taking care of relationships.*"

She remembered the Amish people who lived near her childhood home, and their Memory Quilts that encapsulated family histories. By then, her own mother was dead, but she got in touch with many members of her family, aunts, their daughters, and *their* daughters, ten women in all, and set in motion the largest collaborative web in this enterprise.

Eventually each of the women designed and sewed a section of the quilt. The images are memories from each woman's life. Wright laid them out on a triangular ground symbolizing a mountain; another triangle descending from the "sky" intersects it in a perfect yantra. She added Irish interlace and flowers in appliqué in a rainbow arc over the mountain.

Wright's aunt, Shirley Mitchell Wise of Indiana, spoke for the family about the project. She is a professional dressmaker who had never worked on a quilt; none of the other women involved were particularly interested in needlework. At first they held back "because we weren't sure we had the talent. But we began to be enthusiastic about sharing our lives."

The individual blocks of the quilt were joined with a motif that Mrs. Wise says is a sweetpea vine. Rosemary Wright's mother remembered she'd carried sweetpeas as a bride and that her husband gave them to her on special occasions. It is a vine with long tendrils and long endurance.

Participating family members were: Michelle Wise Alyea, Renee Wise Duncan, Shirley Mitchell Wise, June Mitchell Salzarulo, Annette Salzarulo Rodefeld, Amy Maria Salzarulo, Mary Alice Myers Mitchell, Nancy Mitchell Miller, Kristen Miller, and Jennifer Miller. ★

Members of the Mitchell family showing sections of their quilt. From left (clockwise): Shirley Mitchell Wise, coordinator of Mitchell quilt; June Mitchell Salzarulo; Mary Alice Myers Mitchell; Nancy Mitchell Miller; Renee Wise Duncan.

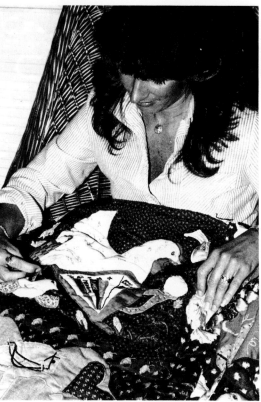

Rosemary Wright at work on designs for The Mitchell Family Quilt.

QUILT TYPE

Repeated images by nonpieced techniques, as photo transfer or painting

ISABEL BISHOP/WENDA F. VON WEISE

FAITH RINGGOLD/WILLI POSEY

VARIATIONS ON THE THEME OF WALKING, II

Isabel Bishop/Wenda F. von Weise

1981, Raw silk and cotton, 76″ x 65″

ORIGINAL ARTWORK
VARIATIONS ON THE THEME OF WALKING
Isabel Bishop, 1978, oil on canvas, 25″ x 32″

The task of translation between any two media entails an understanding of the latent meaning or essence of the original work, how it functions as a vehicle of thought. Isabel Bishop's small painting in transparent oils, measuring about twenty-five by thirty-six inches, is in her characteristic idiom, showing figures walking, swinging their arms, looking straight ahead, in transition, transitory, as if at the crossroads of a city. Wenda von Weise, seeing the painting, even knowing little about Bishop's work, said, "I know!" The image was perfectly suited to a silkscreening process she had developed to transfer color-separated photos onto cloth. The result is a singularly appropriate image: these barely seen, translucent figures caught at a conceptual "intersection" of paint, photography, and cloth.

Bishop's career has been a distinguished one. Raised in the East and Midwest, she found herself at the end of World War I a student at the New York School of Applied Design. Later she attended the Art Students League, and worked with Kenneth Hayes Miller and Guy Pène du Bois. Over the years she developed imagery and painterly style based on the strange nature of light: that transparent radiance that renders solid things visible.

Von Weise, born in Princeton, New Jersey, and educated in New England, did crewel and needlepoint as a young woman and made her own clothes as she shot up to her near-six-foot height. In the 1970s at the Cranbrook Academy of Art and the Cleveland Institute of Art, she studied fiber and photographic processes, and began to think about the typical American family photo-album as a subject for art. Later, when she turned to patchwork quilts, she wondered whether the two media—both "patch-work"—could be combined. Eventually she developed a way of screening photos onto cloth for quilts of her own design, as well as for soft sculpture. Her conceptual works in this mixed-media technique derive as much from the "fine" as the "material" arts; they are imbued with literary meanings that the titles spell out: *I Remember East 118th Street* (1973); *Nantucket Film Strip* (1975); *Fabricated Landscape: Straight Furrows in Geologic Time* (1979). In her teaching workshops, she encourages students to bring in their own photo collections and to move in a sort of pilgrimage from family images to those of landscape. Bishop's image, fulgent with meaning appropriate to this era's spiritual condition, was perfectly suited to the von Weise technique.

She photographed the work and made color separations, representing the four color processes. For transferring the image to the cloth, however, von Weise played with and changed the tones and degrees of saturation, repeating the basic image six times before quilting it on a large frame in the traditional manner.

To Bishop, the project at first seemed a mere curiosity, but in the end she learned from it. "Strange, that in art forms so different, there is this one thing that joins them: *materiality,* the

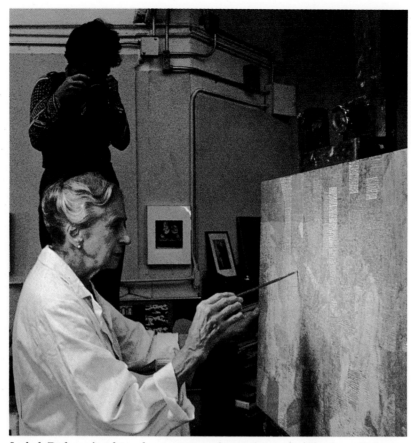

Isabel Bishop finishing her painting for quilt, with Charlotte Robinson (background), 1980.

basic conception of materiality, is the link. In painting, the material aspect is implicit and disguised. The material aspect of a painting can be meant to disappear, actually *not to be there*. But in the quilt, the material aspect is foremost and explicit." The task of the quilter, then, would be to distill from the painting the material element and raise it to the foreground of attention.

In this case, the essential quality of the painting was conveyed by (or simply *was*) the transparency and thinness of the oil glazes and the way these layered deflectors of light, and so of color, functioned. The presented image (of girls walking back and forth, insubstantial in their physical nature and in transit between locations) was really no more than a restatement in another medium of the painting's meaning in terms of pure color. The quilter, in directing her attention to the technical task of rendering the colors appropriately, achieved an uncannily successful translation of the presented image, but by indirect means. In each case, light—composite, paradoxical, and insubstantial—was the "material" at issue. ★

Echoes Of Harlem

Faith Ringgold/Willi Posey

1980, Hand-painted cotton, 100″ x 96″

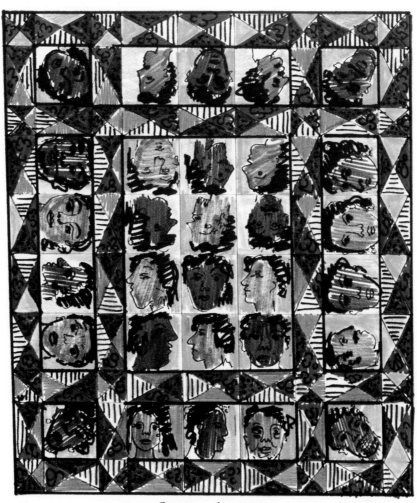

ORIGINAL ARTWORK
ECHOES OF HARLEM
Faith Ringgold, 1979, felt-tip pen on paper, 8½" x 7½"

W illi Posey, born in 1907 in Palatka, Florida, was Faith Ringgold's mother, teacher, guide, quilter, and friend. Her death shortly after finishing this quilt has given both the project and the work a special importance to her daughter. Posey was trained at the Fashion Institute of Technology in New York and became a dressmaker and fashion designer. "She didn't think of herself as an artist but as a businesswoman," says Ringgold. "She had to get the cruise-women ready." As a child, Posey had made a quilt alongside her grandmother in the old way, boiling flour sacks until they were white for the backing. Her own mother, Ida, made one for a baby boy who died, its top satin with pink roses; it stayed in the family a long time. Ringgold once suggested that if she had been left to her own devices and not influenced on the way by mainstream esthetics,

she would have turned to cloth-work earlier. As it was, it took her experience in the Women's Movement of the 1970s to open her eyes to what women in her family had done for generations. Eventually she put together a way of working from many personal sources: flat African images, all-over geometric designs like Tibetan tankas, portraits and doll figures based on real-life characters.

Since the early 1970s, Ringgold has made these cloth figures of people she knows, neighborhood people, famous people. She invented and Posey sewed their clothes. Together mother and daughter set up a small cottage industry: dolls to be marketed in kits. "For every project, she made extras. 'Here are some extras,' she'd say. Extra tankas for instance. 'Someday you'll be making paintings for these extra tankas.' For the doll project, she made a whole chest of clothes. I'll never run out." During the last weeks

*Faith Ringgold painting her design on fabric for Ringgold/
Posey quilt, 1980.*

of her life, Posey obsessively worked and packed the kits. Eventually she had laid up eight hundred of them, while Ringgold kept begging her not to exhaust herself. "I'm finishing my work," said Posey.

But of all these cooperative endeavors, "the quilt was our great work together. We had great gossip! We didn't do any kitchen-talking, we did working-talking. I can't think of anything we didn't say.

"I couldn't have done it alone. I needed my mother. And she would never have collaborated with anyone else. With me, she had a chance to go on being what she was...my mother."

For the quilt, Ringgold dyed muslin a tone that suggested the outdoors, then painted in the faces of men and women, who were her neighbors in Harlem. "It's for a bed, to be laid out flat. These people belong together.

"The quilt covers people. It has the possibility of being part of someone's life forever. It's about harmony."

In the actual making, however, a dispute arose, not surprisingly over a technical point. Posey wanted to cut and stitch the triangles in the border in a certain way. "She must have had a certain quilt in her head, maybe the one her grandmother had done. All 'art people' have images in their heads, images that can't be put into shape easily. I didn't understand, then, that she had that kind of idea.

"Well, at the end, we got the top done, and she lined it, and I put in the tie knots and it was time for the quilting. Her eyes were failing then. She wanted little stitches, and she took off on her own, ignoring the marks I'd made, stitching right across them.... I'm glad that at the end, I could feel free enough to say to her: Okay, yes, go ahead. *Do it your way.*" ★

QUILT TYPE

Miscellaneous abstract/conceptual solutions

Marcia King/Nancy Vogel/Bob Douglas
Marilyn Lanfear/Theresa Helms
Charlotte Robinson/Bonnie Persinger

CANTILEVER

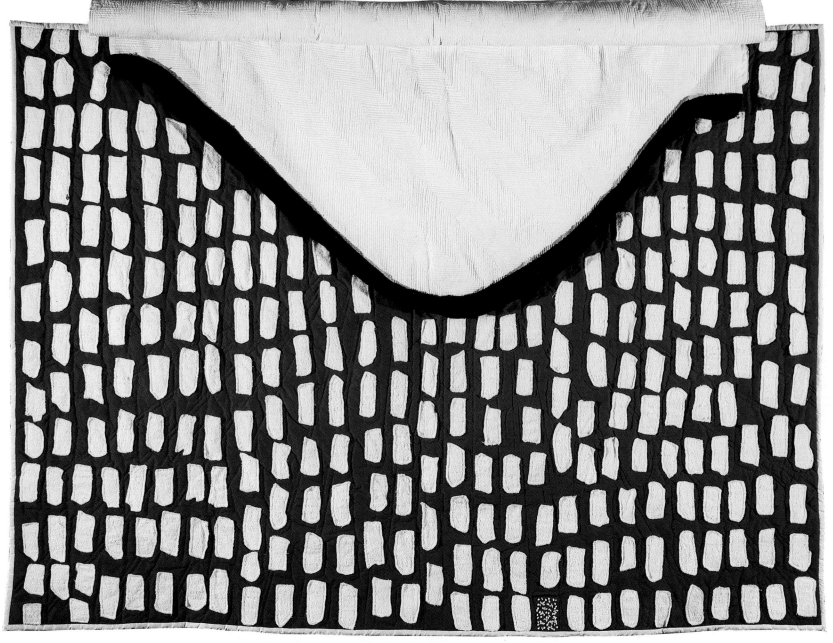

Marcia King/Nancy Vogel/Bob Douglas

1982, Cotton, 77″ x 103″

ORIGINAL ARTWORK
WORKING DRAWING
Marcia King, 1982, acrylic impasto on paper, 22″ x 30″

Marcia King expressed an idiosyncratic sensitivity to certain qualities of cloth as she talked about her quilting project. As she described it, she had searched almost compulsively until she found a fabric that relieved her of nervous distress. For her, the crisscrossing intersections of fibers are what one might call "sites of sensitivity." Her reactions were sharp and could be articulated. She did not like velvets next to silk. She did not like stitchery over velvet. On some fabrics, she liked a French knot; on others, not. What she pressed to discover—not knowing it until it was found—was a tight-woven fabric in which the fiber crossings were smooth. "That sent me . . . it had sheen. With that, the whole quilt fell into shape. I was fascinated that the response was *to the material*, to that beautiful bolt of raincoat fabric: that poplin.

"It was tough. Good. It had elegance. It was so . . . useful." There were numerous small rectangles of terry cloth that were to be aligned across it. Although the terry was effective, until the right ground was found, "It had bothered me. It didn't seem *timeless*. But when I saw the poplin, I knew I had something timeless." That artist's language is full of coded information.

King is a latecomer to professional art life. Raised in Cleveland, Ohio, a graduate of Smith College, she lived for twenty years in San Antonio, Texas, where she began painting, winning recognition almost at once. In 1981 she moved to New York. Living in various places, she had become especially aware of the impact of light on an artist's vision.

Like some European artists who diverged radically from the Impressionists, she has seen her own palette "dulling off." Most bizarrely as well, for a time a textural element infiltrated the tissues of her paintings and some sculptural furniture she was making—"presences" like lamps and bureaus. She began these works by laying white paper disks all over the wood or canvas surfaces. King says the idea came from Mexican "Day of the Dead" figures, speckled to suggest decay. But one can suppose that memories of her chronically ill and steadily worsening father, and his eventual death, are the real root of this strange idiom. Her quilt, with its deep white swag at the top, its heavy black passage beneath the swag, its muted colors and curious play of textures, does convey something of the somber aspect of a deathbed. In that respect it stands out as the most unexpected work in this collection. It is possible, too, that in developing this extraordinary projected and transformed image of a deeply painful experience King freed herself from it. Her recent works are extremely large, dramatically striking images of animals with boldly charged, even dimensional surfaces.

Nancy Vogel has confessed that there were some "hitches" in getting the difficult concept going. However, her use of the word "interpretation" to describe her labor suggests that she thought of it as a joint effort, and that she as "interpreter" did not feel

Marcia King and Nancy Vogel working out design for Cantilever.

constrained, but rather interested. "I had a feel for the work," she says. It was a "great opportunity." King kept trying to explain what she wanted; in the end she sent a paper mockup, and the difficulties were overcome. The worst communication gap came about when King tried to describe the swag as an "ocean wave." There is a traditional quilting pattern by that same name, and Vogel went astray until the linguistic tangle was sorted out. The quilting was done by machine on the swag and by hand—in a great push at the end—on the poplin.

Vogel is the first in her family to do professional creative work, although her mother and grandmother sewed some, and an aunt quilted. As a girl she made clothes for herself and her dolls; she majored in home economics and textiles. She was introduced to quilting by her friend Sharon McKain, with whom she studied in 1972. Later, she also took courses with well-known New York artist/quilters Beth and Jeffrey Gutcheon. Her work now combines traditional techniques with eclectic patterns. Recently she has combined Indian sand painting motifs with sections of mola and "Seminole patchwork." She works on commission, selling to major collections. One of her quilts was presented not long ago to Governor Brown of Kentucky. Lately she has been working on a project called "Warm Windows," designed to conserve heat with quilted window panels. In all this exploration and invention, the gift of manual dexterity is the source of her energy. The continual exercise of that gift, as we know from the examples of many artists, rounds out the whole life. Vogel's father was a woodworker; his workshop was at the back of the house in which she grew up. Now, after many years, Vogel has a friend who is also a woodworker, with whom she is doing collaborative projects. "So I began, and ended up, with a woodworker." ★

A Quilt Is A Cover

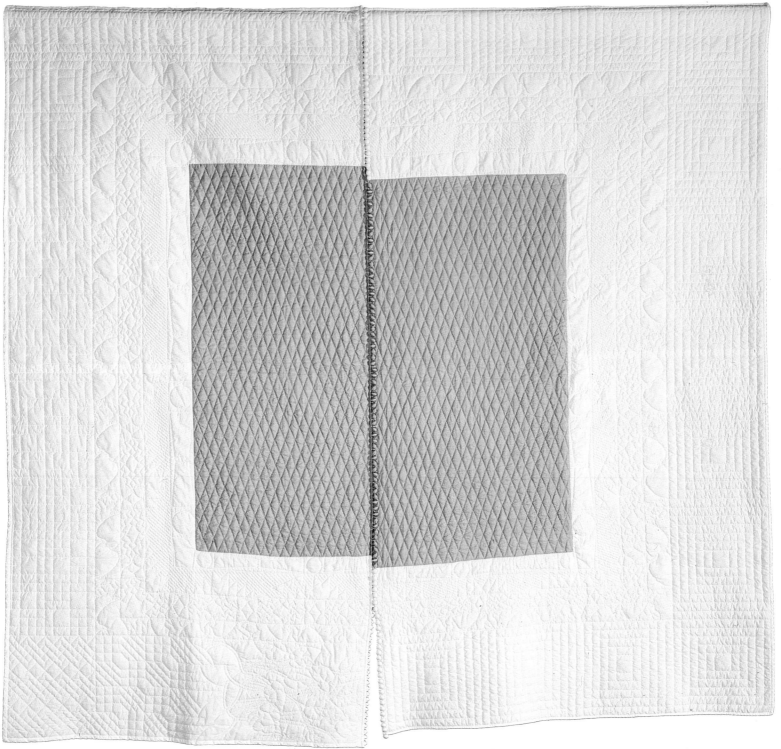

Marilyn Lanfear/Theresa Helms
1981, Cotton and silk, 80″ x 87″

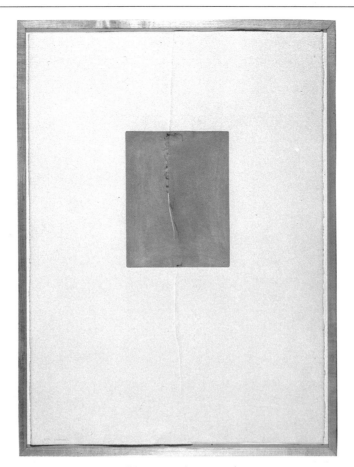

ORIGINAL ARTWORK
DISCHARGE SERIES NO. 2
Marilyn Lanfear, 1980, drawing on paper, 30″ x 22″

This is the most frankly conceptual work in the collection, an object replete with literary meaning, on which not only the collaborating pair, mother and daughter, have left their symbolic signatures, but the other members of the family—husband, two sons, and another daughter—theirs too. It's an "autobiographical work," says Marilyn Lanfear, putting it mildly. And her quilting daughter expands on the arrangement: "We had a close relationship, artist to artist. Instead of saying, 'Here's the art, transfer it to cloth,' it was: 'Let *us* make a quilt that is an art object.'"

Both women grew up among women who sewed. Lanfear's mother could "really do things." On both sides of the family, the women hooked rugs, made all the clothes and quilts. In fact, Lanfear's mother's four-poster bed was fitted with a quilting frame that could be lifted up and let down by pulleys. Such an odd contraption may well have provided the root inspiration for this quilt, historically traditional, clearly a literal bed or frame broken into the spouses' equal but different territories.

These women's lives have included radical "breaks" and adjustments. Lanfear's grandparents traveled from Mississippi/Alabama to Texas by covered wagon. Plantation owners before the Civil War, they lost a world in that tragedy. Thereafter, the family struggled to survive; the women helped by dressmaking. Later, the very day Lanfear's parents moved their household from Waco to Corpus Christi turned out to be Pearl Harbor Day: another war, and displacement in the life of a child. Then Lanfear's mother's death, three years ago, was difficult to accept. "I thought it would have been nice if she'd known about the quilt."

It was not until about sixteen years ago that Lanfear, married and with four children, decided, "If I was calling myself an artist, I'd better begin." She went back to school, receiving her M.F.A. in 1978. The years before had been hard: a young husband in the army; moves from base to base; all those pregnancies; a case of hepatitis; at last, pressured schooling coming to an end, and

Marilyn Lanfear and daughter Theresa Helms with their quilt.

her mother's illness. She was making prints at the time, and looked to them to bear the brunt of her emotion. She would glue papers together, packaging a shiny powder in the middle, then tear the top sheet so the dust would trickle out. "The children were young, growing. Mother was dying. There was a lot of tearing apart..." It was just then that the quilt project came into being. Her first model was a quilt representing an artist's mind "in process," with thick bunches of fabric projecting from it labeled "silk illusion," or "synthetic illusion." But in the end she accepted that a quilt was, essentially, a "cover," and so should be perceived not as process but as object.

The two unequal sides of her design are husband and wife. Theresa Helms sewed a row of tiny wedding-dress buttons down the middle, but purposely misfitted them. If you button them, the edges are off; if the edges fit, the center will not work. The backing of the quilt is of "domestic" fabric, the front of "broadcloth," the center of "silk-faced satin"—to convey the feminist concept of woman as one required to display her charms. The

outer quilted patterns are "courthouse steps" for the husband and for Lanfear, a wobbling pattern traditionally called "drunkard's path." The four children's rows come within: for Theresa, horns, antlers, and hearts; for Genie, who is a dancer, ribbons, bows, and mazes; for Richard, an outdoorsman, mountains and sky; and for Daniel, baseballs and bats.

Both artists have returned to their own individual work since completing the quilt; both make dimensional pieces. Helms, who designs children's clothes, also makes constructions nearly flat to the wall in distressed paper and a metal sandwich-sheet provided by her husband, an electronics engineer. Lanfear has been working on a curious series of women's blouses—made of lead. They are spectral: a dulled gray surface and empty neck-holes as if, as Lanfear says, the spirit had just departed with a sound like "Whoosh...." Like Marcia King's quilt, these works of Lanfear's may be restructurings of events too painful to live with save in the transformed shape of art, yet too important to be abandoned. ★

THE BLUE NILE

Charlotte Robinson/Bonnie Persinger

1982, Cotton and silk, 104″ x 77″

ORIGINAL ARTWORK
WORKING PAINTING
Charlotte Robinson, 1982, acrylic on canvas, 52" x 38"

Charlotte Robinson is descended from a medical family: her father is a pediatrician, her brother a surgeon, and her mother, who died when Charlotte was three, had been a nurse. There was another break in the lifeline anterior to that loss; most of her mother's ties with her family were cut when she went south, to Tennessee, to marry. It was years before Charlotte began to discover samples of her mother's "incredible embroidery" in the house. "Father packed them away in a trunk when she died and kept them till I was married."

Raised by a series of servants, Robinson and her sisters were frequently directed to sit down and cut out pieces for quilts. "We made thousands." Their father's mother taught the girls to darn and sew. Seeing their projects take shape was a growing pleasure, and slowly it was learned that, in the end, the drudgery that had gone into the making was forgotten. Work was "something we just did." Robinson's drive to keep this collaborative project between artists and quilters underway—a heroic task considering she has dealt for seven years with some thirty-five widely separated artists—may reflect her need to bring together the scattered members of a family and make their reunion endure and be fruitful.

When she set out to choose an image for her own quilt, she wanted it to concern, in some way, water and a high, long view of landscape, as if from a plane or a flying cloud. She had, in the course of travels with her engineer husband, traveled the length of the Nile. Back home, she had turned out a body of paintings and drawings based on the river. Now she wanted to push the quilt idiom in a new direction. Of the thousands of quilt patterns she had studied at the Institute of Design of the Smithsonian Institution, not one dealt with the theme of water in a "soft-edge," fluid manner (such traditional patterns as *Ocean Waves, Storm at Sea*, and *Lady of the Lake* interpret the theme in "hard-edged," triangular pieced patterns). The reason has to do with technique: such an image would be built of curves and transparencies, edgeless and insubstantial, and these qualities seemed outside the scope of cloth art. Nevertheless, she presented Bonnie Persinger with such fluid design, in a work measuring about two by three-and-a-half feet, in acrylic washes. In a word, Persinger was "challenged."

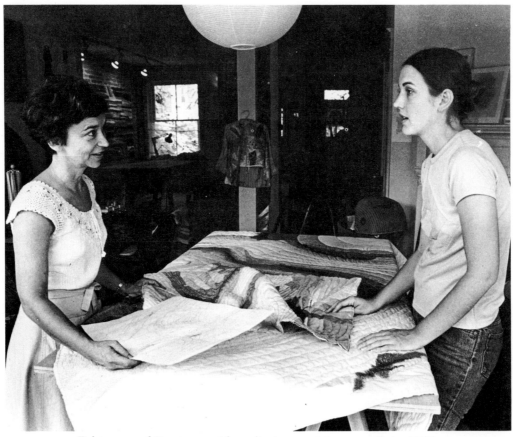

Robinson and Persinger with preliminary miniature quilt in 1977.

"So what I did was work out the major color areas and separate them, deciding where one ended and another began. Eventually I used transparent organdies, with grays overlapping the others. And finally to make the edges merge, I invented an original technique of 'needle painting.' You put the fabric into an embroidery hoop and work it under the machine till the lines of stitches look like brushwork, blurring the edges. And then we started creating whole other shapes...." The work has landscape overtones; its title is *Blue Nile*, and it speaks of origins and distances, sunlight and water.

Both women report that the collaboration has borne fruit far beyond the actual quilt. "Before," says Persinger, "my quilts were innovative but the designs still relied on traditional elements: straight lines dividing distinct color areas, opaque cottons, geometric orderliness. I wanted to push against those limits. I wanted to go beyond the soft-sculpture/quilt *Corn Quilt* I'd made. Working on *Blue Nile* broadened my thinking. Now I work in delicate, interweaving colors. I think my work has taken on new depth. I still make use of flat planes, but I also use curves and transparencies.

"And I think Charlotte's work has developed even more under the influence of the project. If my quilts are more painterly, her paintings are now quiltlike."

If Persinger's work has been enriched, in other words, it may be that Robinson's has become more authoritatively constructivist: she has moved to making large panels with distinct color blocks set in architectural compositions, and even to constructions in canvas, lumber, and fabric. Indeed when she came later to rework the *Blue Nile*, she overlaid the earlier sewn and dyed areas with colors sprayed down just as if they were appliquéd cuts of cloth. Then Persinger went over the hard edges, to soften them with her "needle painting."

In recent years Robinson turned out the series of drawings of her friends' hands that was the inspiration for the quilts on this book's covers and the symbol for a constructive collaboration. These are stopped shadows of women who stood in a circle for a time and then, parting, moved on to their other lives. Three of the participating women have died. But in a "timeless" dimension, the implication is, they make their claim to be remembered. ★

Charlotte Robinson hanging quilts for a photo session.

CHAPTER 5

DESIGN AND CONSTRUCTION:
A Quilters' Notebook

by BONNIE PERSINGER

Illustrations by Daphne Shuttleworth

In 1976 Charlotte Robinson saw one of my quilts in a juried show and approached me about joining the project. Discussions about a quilt project had been ongoing for about a year but no quilt had actually been made. Since Charlotte's work was not at all "quiltlike" in appearance, it was thought that her painting would be a good test case. If we could translate her transparent, blending design into a quilt, then we supposed we would have little difficulty with other artworks that were to be similarly interpreted in a new medium.

The other paintings that were "candidates" for quilts presented a myriad of images. Selection of the first wave of quiltmakers was based on the similarity between their previous work and the styles of the artworks of the artists who were participating in the project. Chris Wolf Edmonds, who had executed a quilt interpretation of a Norman Rockwell painting, seemed to be the foremost "portrait" quilter in the country. Pat Newkirk, a master at drafting patterns and piecing, was the perfect partner for Joyce Kozloff, whose quilt was a pattern of intricate geometric designs. Wenda von Weise's photo-silkscreen quilts suggested a means of interpreting Isabel Bishop's complex work. The sculpture that Betty Parsons selected suggested very heavy fabrics, fabrics that would probably require machine techniques—Amy Chamberlin's specialty. And family members joined together as teams, drawing on a similarity of experience rather than a similarity of style. One artist and her daughter created *A Quilt Is a Cover*, which portrays the story of their family. Another artist and her mother created *The Echoes of Harlem*, a representation and reflection of neighborhood friends. And a large contingent from the Mitchell family gathered together to tell the story of their clan through *The Mitchell Family Quilt*. Certainly geography was a factor in some of the pairings of artist and quilter. It is very hard to collaborate if the two are unable to touch the same fabric; in fact, some pairings nearly failed because of lack of contact.

As the quilters joined the group one by one, we brought our own experiences and talents to the undertaking. Not many had contact with one another until after the quilts were finished. When finally united as a group, experiences were compared, and it was discovered that the quilters, surprisingly, had tackled some problems in similar ways, while others had found uniquely individual solutions for their problems.

There had been no ground rules for collaboration. Each team had divided the work as it saw fit. Some quilters chose the fabrics themselves, later showing them to the artists for approval. This seemed to work well for artists whose existing painting was to be translated; few were not necessarily concerned with how, in particular, this translation would be effected. Several teams, including Harmony Hammond/Bob Douglas, Joyce Kozloff/Patricia Newkirk, and Ellen Lanyon/Angela Jacobi, went together on fabric-buying expeditions, collaborating on important decisions regarding the substance of the quilts. Other artists felt a need to select the material themselves. Lynda Benglis, for example, brought fabrics from India, the source of her inspiration for *Patang*. Elaine Lustig Cohen found all the polished cottons for Sharon McKain—adjusting her design according to the colors of fabrics she found available.

Buying the fabric was just the first step. The next step, for most of the quilters, was working out a pattern for the design—in the proper size. Quiltmakers have traditionally worked out pieced patterns either by folding paper or by drawing on graph paper. Newkirk took the use of graph paper a step further, and used isometric graph paper to work out her pattern. The isometric grid forms diamond shapes that intersect at different angles, which enabled her more easily to draft Kozloff's pattern of intersecting angles.

Several artists worked out full-size drawings of their designs, allowing the quilters to use tracings as pattern pieces; while other designs had to be enlarged. One oft-used method for enlarging appliqué designs is to draw a grid on the small design and then draw a corresponding grid of the desired finished size. The grids are used as guidelines for drawing the larger design. Edmonds used this method for *Olivia in Blue Hat.* A number of other tools for enlargement were also employed. Lanyon used a slide projector to enlarge her design. Parson's, Robinson's, and Dorothy Gillespie's designs were enlarged by using an overhead projector. Bob Douglas enlarged *Fan Lady Meets Ruffled Waters* mathematically, by multiplying each linear dimension by two.

The techniques used to express similar images varied with the materials and the preference of the quiltmaker. Newkirk and McKain machine-pieced geometric patterns; Marilyn Price chose to silkscreen a similar pattern. Judy Mathieson used the English method of basting the fabric over paper before hand-piecing some of her fans. Curved designs were handled in a variety of ways. Edmonds, Jacobi, and the Mitchell family appliquéd their curves; those in *Patang* were machine-appliquéd and in *The Blue Nile,* machine-pieced. Edith Mitchell reached back to tradition, making a Crazy Quilt of *The Road to the*

Center of the World, in which the overlapping colors of satin and embroidery suggest overlapping transparencies. Marie Ingalls also combined a variety of traditional needlework techniques, including hand appliqué and crewel embroidery. Faith Ringgold painted directly on fabric, while Wenda von Weise silkscreened photo-images for *Variations on the Theme of Walking, II.*

Most of the quilting was stitched by hand. Nancy Vogel and Bob Douglas machine-quilted the swag portion of *Cantilever,* for which Vogel had hand-quilted the main area. Chamberlin made both of her quilts on the machine by the "quilt-as-you-go" method. Gillespie's quilt was machine-quilted in one piece after the edges had been carefully basted under; so quilting lines could reach the edges without being inhibited by the binding.

Quilters are conservative when it comes to marking their work, as well they should be. After spending hundreds of hours working on the top of the quilt, no one wants to use any method of marking that would ruin the design. Most of the quilters in this project used lead pencils, although some others used pounce or pins. Only one team mentioned using a new blue marking pen that is supposed to wash out in cold water: Marilyn Lanfear and Theresa Helms, who had never before made a quilt. The marker did indeed wash out, but most quilters seem not to trust such "new-fangled" marking implements.

The many unique and innovative techniques used to create these quilts demonstrate the inventiveness of the participants in the project.

Following is a description of how five of the quilters constructed their quilts. One quilt was chosen from each of the visual categories described by Eleanor Munro in her essay.

AMY CHAMBERLIN

According to Amy Chamberlin, "Lynda's design was inspired by kites seen flying in the skies over India. The fabrics, too, came from India. When I first saw the satins, I didn't like the thought of working with them. Quilts are supposed to be made of sturdy fabrics. But once I started working with them, the reflections fascinated me. I even began adding sparkle with gold thread.

"After I received the fabric and the design, the next step was to enlarge the drawing. To do this, I traced each of the twenty 'blocks,' which in this case were rhombuses— parallelograms with equal sides. I then folded the tracing into thirds, both horizontally and vertically, to establish a grid." A block of the desired finished size was cut from tracing paper and also folded into thirds each way to establish a corresponding grid system in proportion to the original. The designs, from the small blocks, were then drawn onto this larger pattern, using the foldlines as guides.

A tracing of each enlarged design was made. Key marks were placed across the design lines on curves and on other strategic points that needed to be matched precisely. The fabric grain line was also drawn on each piece to help align the pattern on the fabric while cutting. This pattern sheet was cut apart.

The fabric for each piece was placed wrong-side up on the cutting table. The pattern was placed right-side down and pinned to the fabric with the grain lines aligned with the direction of the threads in the fabric. The pattern was traced with a chalk pencil and points that needed to be matched were marked on the fabric piece. Generous seam allowances were added as the piece was cut from the fabric. On edges that would form the outside edges of each block, a one-inch seam allowance was added. Inside curves were staystitched on the machine and the seam allowances were clipped. Light colored fabrics were interfaced with a second layer of cotton fabric to prevent background fabrics and seam allowances from showing through them.

Each block was sewn together on the sewing machine using a combination of patch and appliqué techniques. For some blocks, the background was pieced, then a design appliquéd over it. Other blocks were pieced on one side and curves on the opposite side were appliquéd. For each piece to be appliquéd, a lightweight cardboard template was cut in the shape of the pattern piece. This cardboard pressing template was aligned on the wrong side of the fabric piece and the seam allowances were pressed over the cardboard. The fabrics used in the quilt held a sharp crease easily.

The appliqué stitches used were meant to be as inconspicuous as possible. A fine machine needle, size #65, and size 50 machine embroidery thread were used. The machine was set for a small blind hem stitch. This

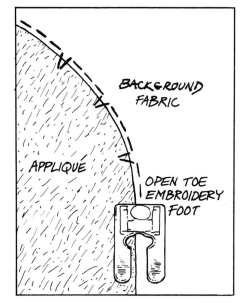

stitch is a series of straight stitches on the right with one zigzag to the left. It produces an almost invisible line of appliqué stitches when the straight stitches fall on the background fabric and the zigzag stitches cross over onto the figure being appliquéd. An open toe embroidery foot was used while stitching, to make guiding the stitches around curves and points easier.

One piece of gold fabric was especially hard to handle, so for the two blocks with the mitered striped background, the appliquéd parts were handled a little differently. For the

large gold shapes, freezer paper with plastic fused to one side was used instead of a pressing template of cardboard. The freezer paper was cut to the pattern shape and then fused in place by pressing it onto the fabric with the plastic side of the paper to the wrong side of the fabric. The seam allowances were then pressed over the edge of this paper. The inner curves had been staystitched and clipped, allowing them to be pressed flat. The seam allowances on outer curves were eased in by running a line of gathering stitches ¼" from the finished edge. A cardboard template was placed on the wrong side and the gathering line pulled, easing the seam allowance into place. Pressing produced a sharp edge on which to apply the appliqué stitching. The stem designs were also pressed over a cardboard template, then pinned to the gold fabric, which still had the paper fused to the back, making it easy to handle. Next, the circle was pressed and stitched onto the gold shape. The gold fabric underneath the circle was trimmed out, leaving a ½" seam allowance. After the gold shape with its appliqués was pinned to the background fabric and stitched in place, the striped background fabric under the gold was also trimmed away.

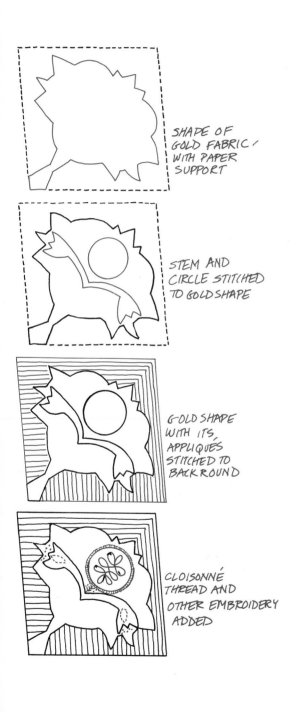

SHAPE OF GOLD FABRIC WITH PAPER SUPPORT

STEM AND CIRCLE STITCHED TO GOLD SHAPE

GOLD SHAPE WITH ITS APPLIQUES STITCHED TO BACKROUND

CLOISONNÉ THREAD AND OTHER EMBROIDERY ADDED

The freezer wrap was removed; it pulled away easily. If it had loosened while working, it would have been fused back in place by re-pressing with an iron.

At this point the gold "cloisonné" thread was added to the circle. To mark the line on which the thread would be stitched, the design was first traced onto wax paper. The wax paper was then placed in the sewing machine and the design stitched with the needle un-threaded. This made a line of holes through which pounce could be rubbed. For pounce, Chamberlin uses either cornstarch or chalk powder wrapped in cotton fabric and secured with a rubber band. After the gold thread was couched on this line, by machine, the ends were pulled to the wrong side with a large-eyed needle.

Once all the blocks were stitched together, the block, batting, and backing fabrics were cut to the same size from a block-size template that included a 3/8″ outer seam allowance. Since the satins used in the quilt were suscep-tible to fraying, the edges were marrowed or overcast. Chamberlin's sewing machine has an overlock foot that helped keep the edge from rolling while overcasting it with a zigzag or overlock stitch. She could have also used a

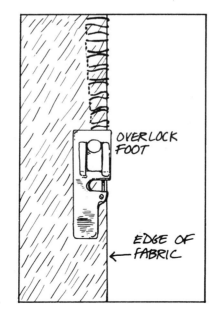

OVERLOCK FOOT

EDGE OF FABRIC

running or serpentine stitch, in which case she would have drawn the cutting line, stitched next to it, then cut along the line.

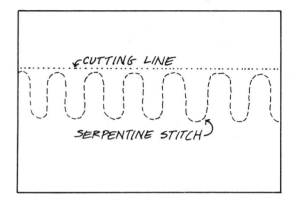

CUTTING LINE

SERPENTINE STITCH

"I was now ready to quilt each block," Chamberlin explains, "matching the top thread to a color in the design and the bobbin thread to the backing. The three fabrics (the top, batting, and backing) were layered to-gether and a pin was placed in each corner. It was easy to pin-baste the blocks when they

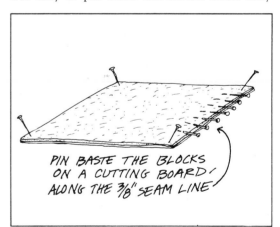

PIN BASTE THE BLOCKS ON A CUTTING BOARD ALONG THE 3/8″ SEAM LINE

were placed on a well-padded cutting board, keeping the block taut by sticking the pins through the layers along the edges and into the board. The layers were pin basted together along the 3/8″ seamline. The pins were placed perpendicular to the seamline so that they could be easily removed as I replaced them with machine basting. Sewing this line first secured the three layers together." This bast-ing could easily be removed later when the blocks were to be joined. After basting around the outside edges, each shape within the block was pin basted and outlined with quilting stitches. These outlines were used to establish other quilting lines. The succeeding rows of stitching were approximately ⅝″ apart and echoed the particular shape of the area being stitched. The other quilting lines were marked by rows of pins that were easily arranged and rearranged to achieve the desired effect. All stitching stopped one inch from the basting line and was completed after the blocks were joined together. The bobbin thread was drawn to the top at the beginning of each row, and each row of stitching was ended at this precise point. Pulling the bobbin thread to the top insured a clean start for each row of stitching. After each area was quilted, the three threads on top were snapped into the eye of a self-threading needle and drawn into the batting. When the needle was pulled back to the surface, the threads were cut, leaving about ¾″ inside the batting. The other bobbin thread was secured in a similar manner.

In some instances, six strands of embroidery floss were used on the bobbin to add lines of heavy stitching. The bobbin tension was decreased to allow the heavier thread to pass through the tension in a normal manner. The block was placed in the machine wrong-side up and this heavy line of stitching was placed

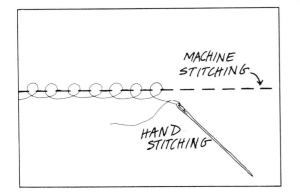

parallel to the rows of quilting already stitched. Other threads were looped through

this stitching by hand after the blocks were finished.

After all the blocks were quilted and embellished with hand and machine embroidery, the blocks were then assembled in a "quilt-as-you-go" method. First, the row of machine basting that circled the block was removed. Then the backing on one block was pinned back so it would not be caught in the stitching. All three layers of a second block were aligned with the two remaining layers of the first block, and pinned with right sides together. The two blocks were joined by stitching along the ⅜″ seamline with the batting side of the first block facing the bed of the machine. After stitching, the seam allowance of the batting was trimmed out close to the line of stitching. The unstitched backing piece was then turned under and whipstitched by hand along the line of machine stitching. Quilting was stitched on both sides of this line to compress the seam allowances and give a uniform look to the quilt. The quilting lines that had stopped one inch from the edge were then completed, their ends again secured by being pulled into the batting. Strips of blocks were then sewn to each other.

Chamberlin recalls: "Lynda sent a piece of wildly striped fabric to be used as binding for the quilt. I felt that, by itself, it competed too strongly with the quilt, so I added a solid color strip of bias cording to separate it from the quilt." The binding was also cut on the bias.

Although the quilt is pieced, appliquéd, embroidered, and quilted by machine, there are many hand stitches. Most of the decorative stitches were added by hand, including the gold threads and embroidery floss that are pulled through the machine stitches to enhance the various motifs. "Machine stitched" implies speed; however, this was not a speedily executed quilt. The nature of the design, the handling of the fabrics, as well as the extra finishing touches all required much time. "However," comments Chamberlin "it was a joy to work with as I watched it come to life and soar."

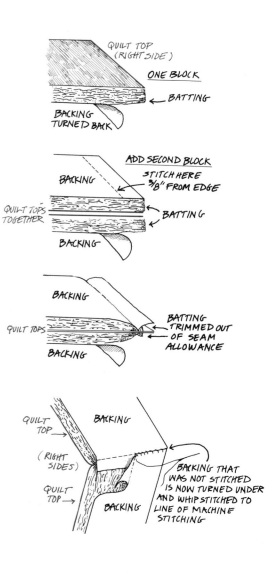

BOB DOUGLAS

Bob Douglas had been working on the fringes of the quilt project for a couple of years. She had quilted the cover quilts and *The Mitchell Family Quilt*, and helped Marcia King resolve a problem with her piece by quilting a bolster to add to the swag Nancy Vogel had made. But until 1982, Douglas had not made any quilt from start to finish. As the last artist was added to the show, Bob seemed the perfect candidate for the job of interpreting her work.

Harmony Hammond and Douglas met on a rainy day in New York. They discussed their previous work, then spent the day seeking fabrics for the project. The painting Hammond had chosen, *Fan Lady Meets Ruffled Waters*, features two characters she frequently uses in her work. Fan Lady, the figure on the left, has an oval body with a fan for a head. Ruffled Waters is the fan-shaped figure leaping toward her from the right.

Hammond worked out an intricate quilting pattern to fill the purple background; it echoes the braided border, but on a smaller scale. A pyramid of horizontal braids meets a sky of vertical braids; each strip is an inch wide.

Douglas meticulously enlarged the tracing Hammond had given her by multiplying all linear dimensions by two. The tiny quilting design was drawn on the purple with a lead pencil. "Then," sighed Douglas, "came the days and days and days of quilting the purple

to turn it into a richly textured background for the figures." The braided border was pieced by hand, then pinned on and sent to Hammond for evaluation. Ruffled Waters was also pieced together and sent along with samples of how Fan Lady might be done.

Fan Lady had been a problem throughout the design phase. How could Douglas achieve the soft blending of the white and black spirals? Having experimented with several different techniques, she sent samples of the more successful ones. These included machine-zigzagging solid bands of both black and white, hand appliquéing black over white, appliquéing both black and white over a base fabric, and embroidering the coils by hand. She even tried building a loop pile by using the tailor-tacking foot on the sewing machine, which leaves a ¼″ high trail of thread loops behind it. Douglas had rejected this method because it looked too much like a giant caterpillar. Along with the samples, Douglas sent Hammond a cardboard template of the size Fan Lady was supposed to be. The quilt design had been very carefully enlarged, but at the larger scale, Douglas thought Fan Lady looked bulky when compared to the other figure. When Hammond saw the quilt she agreed, and Fan Lady was scaled down.

Neither Douglas nor Hammond felt that any of the Fan Lady experiments had been very successful. While contemplating this,

Douglas saw a mola, an intricate reverse-appliqué design from Panama, at Marcia King's studio, and suggested that they use this technique. Hammond had trouble visualizing it until she spotted a similar spiral in a photo of a mola on the back of a newspaper clipping someone had sent her. They agreed that this was the solution.

Douglas constructed the mola-like spiral, varying the width of the strips to avoid too much regularity. She had planned to add large embroidery stitches in a soft, heavy white thread across the black areas to soften the contrast between black and white. But as Douglas and Hammond studied the figure after the appliqué was finished, they decided that the loose stitches used to baste the fabrics together for appliqué provided just the right contrast to the tightly controlled appliqué stitches—so they left the basting stitches in.

Fan Lady and Ruffled Waters were quilted individually. The spots of Ruffled Waters, which Hammond refers to as "spirit dots", were cut out freely, without a pattern, although the rest of the quilt had been very precisely enlarged. The spots were appliquéd onto Ruffled Waters after she was quilted. The two figures were then appliquéd on top of the quilted background, so they seem to hover over the densely quilted purple field.

Douglas and Hammond decided to add an embroidered title across the top and their initials in the lower corners. After seeing all the textures, Hammond also decided she wanted embroidery around Ruffled Waters to soften the edge between the figure and the background. Douglas remembers, "I have this crazy quilt that was made in the 1870s. It was my grandmother's. I borrowed a stitch from it to use on Ruffled Waters. The stitch is very Victorian and ornate. I love this quilt now that I've finished. When I first started, I hated the thought of all that quilting, but all those days spent hunched over the quilting frame have really paid off. All the textures in the quilt have made it richer and richer—like a tapestry."

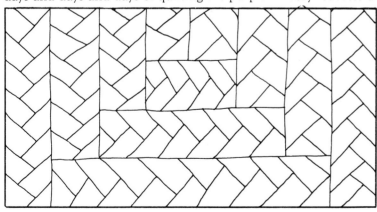

½-SIZE PATTERN OF QUILTING LINES ON BACKGROUND OF QUILT (DETAIL)

ACTUAL-SIZE
DETAIL OF QUILTING LINES
AND STITCHING.

MARILYN PRICE

Marilyn Price's collaboration with Miriam Schapiro began with phone conversations about their work and possible techniques they could use on their quilt. The artists exchanged slides of their work through the mail, and Price sent samples of silk-screened fabric, appliqué, and quilted layers to Schapiro. They finally met to discuss techniques and approaches. Only after this mutual probing into each other's talents and expectations did Schapiro begin to work out the design concept.

"Then in July 1981 I met with Miriam in her East Hampton studio to see the painted model," recalls Price. "I received several aids, including paint swatches for the Baby Block pattern, a template for the quilting grid, a full-size paper pattern for the heart, and lots of inspiration!" The quilting template that Schapiro had made echoed the pattern of the Baby Block portion. The paint swatches were the colors Price would need to achieve for the silk-screened block pattern. Schapiro explained to Price that as she paints, she builds layers, adding pattern on top of pattern. It was important that the quilt be built of layers as well. So as Price made samples of the silk-screened Baby Block pattern, she started the process of layering, by screening the pattern onto subtle printed fabrics, including some tiny calicoes. These bright calicoes threatened to be too dominant, so they were turned over and screened on the wrong side, allowing only a ghost of the pattern to show through. Samples were made on four different fabrics, with various intensities of pigment used on each fabric. Schapiro chose the white cotton flocked with an eyelet pattern, printed with full strength color.

Silk-screening is done with a screen that has been prepared so that the design area is open, allowing the dye to pass through it, while the background area is blocked out. Designs can be applied to the screens in different ways; for instance, by direct painting or photo-transfer. (Price simply used contact-paper stencils applied directly to the screen.) The screen is aligned on the fabric, then dye is placed on the screen and pulled across the design with a squeegee, forcing the dye through the openings in the screen, depositing it on the fabric beneath. With some dyes, more intense color can be achieved by a second application.

Six different screens were used for this quilt, including one each for the black, purple, pink, and cream of the block pattern. Two other, small screens were used for applying the smaller patterns to the diamond shapes that made the blocks. These patterns were made using small templates manufactured for making quilting designs. One is a traditional running feather, the other a lily-of-the-valley pattern. Schapiro uses these templates to stencil designs onto her paintings. Price used them in the quilt by screening the feather pattern in dark purple over the purple section of each

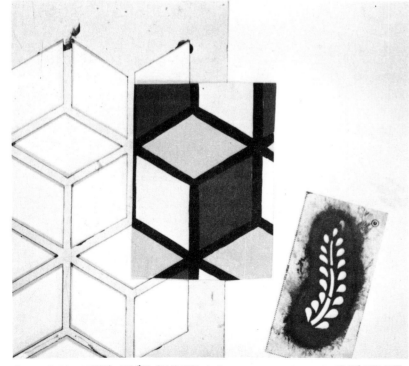

PAPER PATTERN, COLOR SWATCH, AND SMALL TEMPLATE USED TO CREATE LAYERS OF PATTERNS AND COLORS.

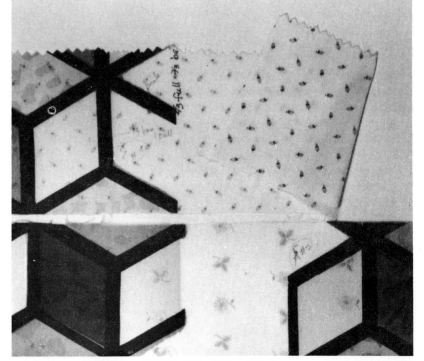

SAMPLES OF FABRIC SWATCHES SHOWING EXPERIMENTS WITH INK STRENGTHS, FABRIC CHOICES, AND USE OF RIGHT- AND WRONG-SIDES.

OUTLINE OF THE TRADITIONAL PATTERN, RUNNING FEATHER, MADE FROM THE SMALL TEMPLATE.

block and the lily-of-the-valley in dark pink over the pink portion. With these designs, still another pattern was layered onto the cloth. "I sent the patterned heart to Miriam. She pinned on the fabric flowers and sent a tracing indicating the outline of the black center. Next came the hardest part—appliquéing the flowers. Miriam had cut them out as she would for collage, leaving no seam allowance. The tightly woven ones could still be appliquéd by hand, turning under just a small amount. But the coarsely woven ones were already unraveling, so I machine-appliquéd them. I had a lot of trouble with puckering while I zigzagged them, so I slipped tissue paper underneath the bottom fabric. It helped a lot." The heart with flowers was then appliquéd to the black background.

The quilting pattern was marked with a soft lead pencil. The quilting design expands the block pattern from the appliquéd heart onto the background. "I found five quilters—Carol Clemonds, Mary Kay Horn, Virginia Koeler, Beryl Poland, and Janet Robertson—to help with hand-quilting. It was really nice to work in a group for this last part of the quilt. We didn't have any trouble working on the black. We usually worked in daylight, and with the contrasting red thread, you could see right away if you had a problem."

This quilt was built entirely of design elements borrowed from traditional quilts, but each element was used in a very different way. The heart, the Baby Block pattern, the running feather and lily-of-the-valley templates were used in a contemporary and original way to produce a quilt that borrows from tradition but is not limited by it.

THE BABY BLOCK PATTERN FROM THE APPLIQUED HEART IS EXTENDED ONTO THE BLACK BACKGROUND IN A QUILTING PATTERN.

WENDA F. VON WEISE

"Isabel Bishop's painting is not easily reproduced by the traditional appliqué, embroidery, or pieced techniques of quiltmaking," noted Wenda von Weise, explaining why she was the right quiltmaker to interpret Bishop's painting. "However, the painting and, of course, any photograph of it are reproducible by commercial printing techniques. These techniques can be used on fabrics, using photographic screen-printing methods."

First, Bishop's painting was photographed through three special filters, each of which blocked different light waves in the color spectrum. One photo was also taken without filters. These four photographs were used to make large (two-by-three-feet) film transparencies. The high-contrast film used to make these transparencies "sees" only black or white. Therefore, gray areas are seen as irregular blotches of black on a white (or clear on the actual film) background. This gives a different effect than the more familiar halftone transparencies. (Halftones are photos made of dots like photos used in newspapers, where the density of the dots determines the shade of gray. Von Weise screened the hands for the cover quilts using halftones of the hand photos.) For Isabel's quilt, von Weise would use the four color-separation transparencies. Theoretically, if these four images were printed in exact registration in the commercial colors of yellow, magenta, cyan, and black, they would exactly reproduce Isabel's painting. Wenda explains, "However, I was interested in interpreting the painting in a quilt format, not duplicating it at another scale." So she used slightly different colors in various combinations. The painting's dominant colors are orange, turquoise, and purple,

so these three colors plus yellow were printed in two- and three-color combinations for each block.

First, four screens were prepared, each printed with the image of one of the color separations. The screens were coated with light-sensitive photographic emulsion, in a darkened room, and allowed to dry. Then a positive film transparency of the exact size of the image to be printed (two-by-three-feet, in this case) was put in direct contact with the screen and exposed to ultra-violet light. The areas not exposed to light, those covered by the black part of the transparency, remained soft. The areas that received light hardened. When the screen was washed out with water, the soft areas washed away, leaving open areas on the screen through which dye could pass during the printing process. The developed screens were allowed to dry.

Next, von Weise pinned the fabric to the printing table, and placed a screen on top of it. Putting a small amount of the dye at one end of the screen, she pulled a squeegee across the screen, forcing the dye through the areas of the screen that were open. She screened the blocks with different colors, using different combinations of the four screens, allowing the fabric to dry after each application of dye. Some blocks were screened in two colors, others in three.

In Bishop's painting *Variations on the Theme of Walking, II* the images of people are walking, quickly passing each other, partially obscured. Their fleeting shadows are barely discernible, at once there and not there. Von Weise's interpretation of this painting perhaps intensifies the intent of the original. Layers of the image are separated and recombined with other layers. The passing shadows are further obscured, each block showing a different focus. Von Weise explains her interpretation: "Each block is approximately the size of Isabel's original painting, and no block is an exact color reproduction of the painting. It is all six blocks seen together that interpret the spirit of Isabel Bishop's painting."

WITH THE FILTERS USED IN THE FOUR-COLOR SEPARATION PROCESS (YELLOW AND CYAN ARE SHOWN AS SAMPLES) AND HIGH CONTRAST FILM, THIS ARTWORK IS CREATED.

BONNIE PERSINGER

Charlotte Robinson's painting was executed in translucent acrylic washes, one color softly merging into another in a composition of gently sweeping curves. To translate this into fabric and thread, we first needed to decide where the edges of the colors were: that is, where one piece of fabric would end and another begin. Charlotte began this process by making an eight-by-ten inch drawing of the painting, in which color areas were a little more defined. I then overlayed this drawing with a piece of translucent Mylar. By tracing the color shapes on the

MYLAR OVERLAY LINE DRAWING USED TO ENLARGE WITH OVERHEAD PROJECTOR.

Mylar, each ultimate fabric shape was defined. Each piece was numbered to make the master "map" showing where each pattern piece would be placed.

The next step was to find fabrics in the colors and values represented in the painting. Because it was impossible to find exactly the colors needed, transparent organdies were used to achieve the very gradual color

changes. For instance, blue organdy over blue cotton fabric would be placed next to two layers of blue organdy over white, followed by one layer of blue organdy over white. In this way, dark blue gradually blended down to pale blue. At the top of the quilt, merging shapes were duplicated by sewing many shapes together and then overlaying these with gray organdy.

I traced the Mylar pattern onto plain white paper, numbered the pieces, and cut it apart to make a pattern for a small mock-up of actual fabric pieces. A fabric color may look perfect when compared to the drawing, but when it is actually placed into the design, it may not work with the other fabrics. So it was important to see each piece of fabric in the

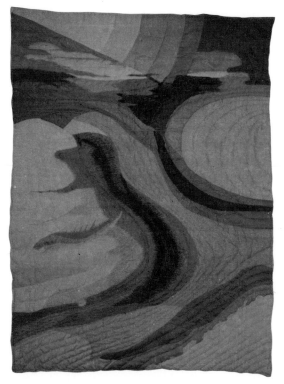

shape and location it would have in the final design. I met with Charlotte to show her the mock-up, changing a few pieces here and there.

She was shocked by the bare skeleton of the model and doubted that we could make the

colors merge. I had an idea for stitching with free-needle machine embroidery over the seamlines to soften these demarcation lines and introduce more mixing of colors. This stitching was to be a major element in the quilt, so in order for us to work out where it

would go, I made a small quilt that was twice the size of the mock-up. Machine embroidery is nearly impossible to remove and the small quilt enabled us to work out small problems that would have become major crises if we had worked on the actual quilt first.

I was now ready to construct the full-size quilt. I enlarged the pattern, using the translucent Mylar and an overhead projector. On a large piece of paper, I drew the finished outline of the quilt and lines dividing it into quarters; the Mylar also had quarter marks. I tacked the paper to the wall and positioned the projector so that the desired area of Mylar was projected onto the corresponding area of paper. The outline and quarter marks helped make certain that the image was not distorted

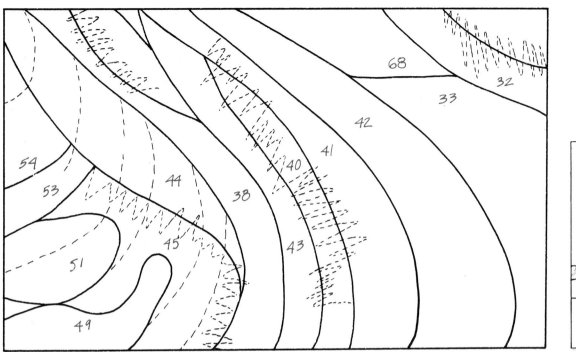

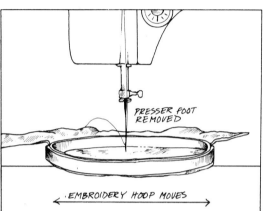

DETAIL FROM COLOR CHART / SHOWS ALSO QUILTING LINES AND ZIG-ZAG STITCHING PLANNED.

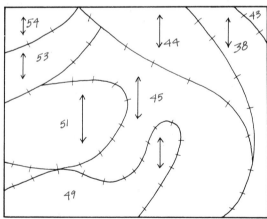

DETAIL FROM COLOR CHART / ALSO SHOWS EACH PIECE MARKED WITH GRAINLINE OF FABRIC AND NOTCH MARKS FOR SEWING PIECES TOGETHER.

by the angle of projection. After tracing the pattern, one quarter at a time, I numbered the pieces to conform to the master. To further prepare the pattern pieces, I marked the grain line on each and made notch marks along the seamlines every twelve inches or so. The notches would help align the pieces for sewing them together later. More notches were needed in areas of very sharp curves, fewer on large straight seams. Each piece was also labeled with its color.

The pattern was then cut apart, and pattern pieces were placed right-side down on the wrong side of the fabric, aligned with the grain. The pattern edge was outlined in pencil; notches were also marked with pencil. The piece was then cut out a ¼″ away from this line.

I was concerned that the sheer fabrics would fray, so I took one additional precaution to ready the fabric pieces before assembly: I cut iron-on interfacing into bias strips just less than one ¼″ wide, ironing these onto the seam allowances as reinforcement. (It worked well. When Charlotte reworked the quilt, it received much more wear and washings than I had ever imagined it would. None of the seams pulled out.)

I machine-pieced the quilt, matching notches and stitching along the pencil lines, then pressed the seams to the inside curves. I then added machine embroidery. To machine embroider, the fabric is placed in an embroidery hoop. The outer hoop is placed on a surface; the fabric is laid over this, right-side up; then the inner hoop is pressed inside (this is opposite from how the hoop is positioned for hand embroidery). The presser foot is taken off the machine, the tensions loosened, and the feed dogs dropped or covered so that the machine cannot move the fabric. The hoop is then moved freely, by hand, in order to direct the stitching. The speed of the movement determines the size of the stitches. Embroidery stitching was applied to seamlines, matching the colors of the two adjacent fabrics, in an attempt to soften, or merge, these lines. In some areas of the quilt, where just a touch of color was needed, it was added with embroidery thread. In other areas, this hint of color was achieved by using a piece of fabric in the accent color with solid embroidery over it in the dominant color, allowing just traces of the fabric color to show through.

The quilt was quilted by hand using rather large stitches, as small stitches would have created a dotted line on which the more fragile fabrics would tear. The quilting lines were rather freeform and did not need much marking. When some guidance was needed, I stuck straight pins in the pattern I wanted as the quilt was stretched in the frame. This guaranteed that no markings would show.

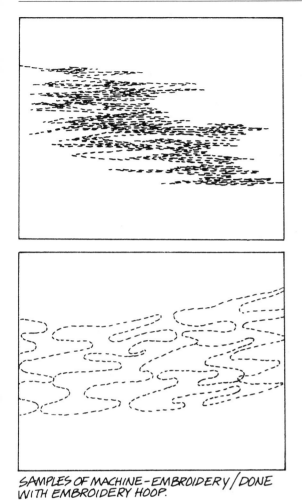

SAMPLES OF MACHINE-EMBROIDERY/DONE WITH EMBROIDERY HOOP.

The quilt was finished and for a few years following its completion it was used as an inspirational example to get others (quilters, painters, museums) interested in the show. During these years, Charlotte's style of painting changed a lot and she felt a strong need to change the design. She thought that perhaps I could appliqué a piece here or there; she could spray textile paint over one area and I could add a border. Well, she started spraying and one thing led to another and we ended up redoing the whole quilt.

In order to spray the areas to be changed, she blocked off areas with masking tape so that paint would not spray on areas where it was not wanted. Then, after mixing the paint and straining it through nylon stockings several times to remove lumps and bubbles, she would spray a small area. If, after unmasking, the color was not right, it could be washed out

if it was still wet. The only other way to change a painted area was to paint over it in another color. Charlotte painstakingly painted each color, toning down the upper area of the quilt and intensifying the center. After a couple of weeks of nonstop spraying, her right hand was so badly strained that it had to be bandaged with a splint. But she went on to finish the quilt, painting for three more weeks with her hand bandaged. When she finished painting, the quilt was tumbled in the dryer in order to set the paint.

I planned to add more embroidery to tie the newly worked areas in with the unchanged sections. To do this I had to "unquilt" the quilt. This was necessary anyway, since the paint had seeped through to the back in many areas. The stitches were difficult to remove because the paint glued them to the fabric. However, the three layers were successfully separated; the original batting and back were thrown out. I embroidered the top. In areas of thick paint, the machine wanted to skip stitches because the fabric was so stiff. I overcame this problem by using a darning spring instead of following my customary practice of using no presser foot. Finally, I added the border and prepared to quilt again.

The quilt top was badly out of shape from repeated stretching and launderings during the painting process. To block it back into shape, I first steam-pressed it over a gridded pressing table. The three layers were then basted together and quilting began again. The original quilting lines had to be reused because there was no paint under the stitches. Each stitch had to cover the exact space it had previously covered. In addition to these quilting lines, it was necessary to add more. Each quilting line added to a quilt shrinks the quilt slightly because fabric that had previously lain flat rolls into the valley formed by the quilting stitch. One reason that quilts are usually quilted with evenly spaced quilting lines is so that the quilt will shrink down evenly—it should remain a true rectangle. If one end of a quilt were closely quilted and the other end quilted with widely spaced lines, the end with the narrowly spaced lines would end up smaller than the other end. This phenomenon was used to cure a problem with

Charlotte's quilt. After pressing, some sections remained that were badly stretched and ballooned above the rest of the quilt. In order to pull these areas down and make the quilt appear flat again, small sections of dense quilting were stitched. They add a special dimension to the quilt and I'm glad they were necessary. Normally, great care would have to be used while designing a quilt using areas of very dense quilting, or one would end up with a misshaped quilt.

The first quilt looked very much like the painting, but eventually the quilt demanded a life of its own. The change in scale demanded a more intense image. So although the painting inspired the quilt, the quilt developed into a separate image of its own.

In the end, each collaboration produced a work of art that is independent of the painting, drawing, or sculpture that inspired it. Each element of the design was studied in minute detail with the choice of line, color, and scale reexamined. The texture of quilting lines also had to be considered. A few artists very carefully planned the quilting pattern to be an integral part of the design, but others found it difficult to incorporate this texture into their usual imagery. The products of this collaborative analysis are a group of quilts that made possible the realization of a new medium for many of the artists, and a broadening of scope and originality of design for the quilters.

I have found that many people, even those who have only a mild interest in art, respond very strongly and emotionally to the quilts in this collection. Part of this appeal, perhaps, may come from their memories of quilts—their associations with home, warmth, security, and comfort. Quilts are made of the materials of everyday life, the same fabrics as our shirts, sheets, and dresses. Unlike the materials of traditional art (canvas, stone, metal), the materials of quilts are warm, soft, and caressing. Instead of viewing them from an emotional distance, we are immediately drawn to them. I rarely see someone touch a painting—but, people cannot keep their hands off a quilt.

BIOGRAPHICAL
INFORMATION

ARTISTS

ALICE BABER

Alice Baber was born in Charleston, Illinois; she spent her childhood in Illinois and near the Everglades in Florida. She studied painting at Indiana University and the Fontainebleau School of Art in France. In 1951 she moved to New York City. After her first solo show in 1958, she lived in Paris and New York for two years. She has traveled widely, most recently to Latin America. Baber's works have been exhibited worldwide; she has had solo shows in the Kunstverein, Cologne, in 1966 and in the Santa Barbara Museum in 1976. She is represented in the permanent collections of the Metropolitan Museum, the Guggenheim Museum, and the Corcoran Gallery of Art, among others. She has taught at the School of Visual Arts, Queens College, New York; and the Universities of Minnesota and California; in 1979 Artist-in-Residence at the Tamarind Institute, University of New Mexico. She died in October 1982.

LYNDA BENGLIS

Lynda Benglis was born in Lake Charles, Louisiana. She went to New Orleans to study art at Sophie Newcomb College of Tulane University, and then moved to New York in 1965, when she was a Max Beckman Fellow. She began working part-time at Bykert Art Gallery while exploring ideas in a basement studio on the Lower East Side. By 1969 she was exhibiting her work. She was a Guggenheim Fellow in 1975 and a National Endowment for the Arts grant recipient in 1979. She has recently completed two large commissions for the Atlanta Airport and the Albany Federal Building. Throughout her artistic career, Lynda has taught at numerous colleges and art schools as a visiting artist. She is represented in the permanent collections of the Museum of Modern Art, the Whitney Museum, and the Guggenheim Museum. Benglis lives and works in New York City and has recently spent time traveling and working in India.

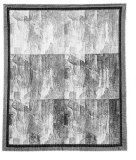

ISABEL BISHOP

Born in Cincinnati, Ohio, Isabel Bishop studied at the New York School of Applied Design and the Art Students League, where she studied with Kenneth Hayes Miller and Guy Pène du Bois. Since 1926 she has had a studio on New York's Union Square, where she and other artists of the Square (Miller, Reginald Marsh, Raphael Soyer, Armin Landeck) became known as the Fourteenth Street School. Bishop was elected to the National Academy of Design in 1940 and to the National Institute of Arts and Letters in 1943; in 1946 she became a vice president of the latter, the first woman officer in the institute's history. She had a one-woman retrospective at the Whitney Museum in 1975 and was presented the Outstanding Achievement in the Arts Award by President Carter in 1979. Her works may be found in the permanent collections of the Metropolitan Museum of Art, the Whitney Museum, the Brooklyn Museum, the New York Public Library, the Hirshhorn Museum, the National Museum of American Art, the Phillips Collection, and many others.

ELAINE LUSTIG COHEN

Elaine Lustig Cohen was born in Jersey City, New Jersey. She studied at Newcomb College, Tulane University, and received her B.F.A. from the University of Southern California. With her husband, Alvin Lustig, she practiced commercial design from 1948 until his death in 1955. From 1955 to 1967 she continued as a freelance graphic designer. The first of her many exhibitions at the John Bernard Meyers Gallery in New York was held in 1970. She has since exhibited at the Galerie Denise René, New York; Mary Boone, New York; Modernism, San Francisco; and Kanus Gallery, Los Angeles. In 1980 she was included in the exhibitions *American Painting: The Eighties* at the Grey Gallery, New York University; *Geometric Abstraction*, Bard College; and *Eight Painters*, Jersey City Museum. In 1981 she exhibited at the Nina Freudenheim Gallery, Buffalo, New York. Her work is represented in many public and private collections.

MARY BETH EDELSON

Mary Beth Edelson was born in East Chicago, Indiana. She studied at the Art Institute of Chicago and DePauw University, and received her M.A. from New York University. A lecturer and artist, she has exhibited both within the United States and abroad. Her one-woman shows include exhibitions at the Albright-Knox Gallery, Indianapolis Museum, Carnegie-Mellon, Corcoran Gallery of Art, and Elise Meyer, Max Hutchinson, and A.I.R. galleries of New York City. Her work has also been in many group exhibitions, including shows at the Haag Gemeentemuseum in Amsterdam; Museu da Arte Contemporanea da Universidade de São Paulo; Galerie Bucholz, München; Whitney Museum of American Art, Fairfield County; Aldrich Museum, Ridgefield, Connecticut; Brooklyn Museum; N.A.M.E. Gallery, Chicago; and the National Collection of Fine Arts; it has also been featured and reviewed in many journals, including *Art forum*, *Flash Art*, *Art in America*, *Arts*, and *Ms.*, as well as in numerous books. She is author of *Seven Cycles: Public Rituals*, and chapters in *The Politics of Women's Spirituality* and *Women's Renaissance*. Edelson has served as visiting artist and lecturer at numerous museums and universities, including the Whitney Museum of American Art, the Art Institute of Chicago, San Francisco Art Institute, and Northwestern University.

DOROTHY GILLESPIE

Dorothy Merle Gillespie was born in Roanoke, Virginia. She studied at the Maryland Institute College of Art in Baltimore, the Art Students League in New York, and at Stanley William Hayter's Atelier 17. Her paintings and sculpture are part of the permanent collections of the Kessel Museum in Germany; Helena Rubenstein Pavilion, Tel Aviv Museum; Frankfurt and Darmstadt Museums in Germany; San Marcos University, Lima, Peru; University of Miami, Florida; and Fordham University, New York. Her work has been on view at individual and group exhibitions, including shows at the Virginia Museum of Fine Art in Richmond, the New York Cultural Center, and the San Francisco Museum. She served as co-coordinator of the Women's Interart Center, at the Fine Arts Museum, and was director of the Art and Community Institute, New School for Social Research in New York.

Harmony Hammond

Harmony Hammond was born in Chicago, Illinois; she has lived in New York City since 1969. Her work has been exhibited in solo and group exhibitions at the Lerner-Heller Gallery, the A.I.R. Gallery, the Nancy Hoffman Gallery in the Downtown Whitney Museum, the New Museum, New York City; the Klein Gallery, Chicago; and Rutgers University, New Jersey. In 1981 the Women's Art Registry of Minnesota and the Glen Hanson Gallery in Minneapolis co-organized a ten-year retrospective of her work. Her art is in numerous public collections, including the Denver Museum of Fine Art, the Walker Art Center, and the Indianapolis Museum of Fine Art. She has taught at many universities and art schools, among them the University of New Mexico, the University of North Carolina, the University of Virginia, and the Tyler School of Fine Art, and has been the recipient of several fellowships, including one from the National Endowment for the Arts and a New York State Creative Artists Public Services Award.

Marcia Gygli King

Marcia King was born in Cleveland, Ohio. She received a B.A. from Smith College. From 1956 to 1960 she was a docent at the National Gallery of Art. Following this, she moved to San Antonio, Texas, where she lived for twenty years. Early in her artistic career she competed extensively, winning a string of top prizes throughout the region. Exhibitions have included six one-woman shows in Washington, D.C., and the Southwest, with a retrospective at the McNamara O'Connor Museum, Victoria, Texas. King was the first visual arts critic in San Antonio, for *Express News*. While she was earning her M.F.A. from the University of Texas at San Antonio, awarded in 1980, she also lectured for the university. In 1981 she moved to Manhattan, New York. Her first one-woman show in the East was held the same year, in the Rutgers University Women Artists Series.

Joyce Kozloff

Joyce Kozloff was born in Somerville, New Jersey. She received her B.F.A. from Carnegie Institute of Technology in 1964 and her M.F.A. from Columbia University in 1967. She has lived in New York City, with periodic absences, since 1964, and has taught at a number of colleges. She has been active in the feminist movement, first in Los Angeles in 1970 to 1971, and thereafter in New York, where she is an associate member of the Heresies Collective. Kozloff has exhibited throughout the United States and in Europe. Her work has evolved from pattern painting, in the early 1970s, to decorative installations, and more recently to architectural ornament for public spaces. Currently she is working on commissions for the Harvard Square subway station in Cambridge, Massachusetts; a subway station in Buffalo, New York; the Wilmington, Delaware, Amtrak Station; and the new international terminal at the San Francisco airport. Public collections housing her works include the Brooklyn Museum, the Museum of Modern Art, the Metropolitan Museum of Art, and the National Gallery of Art.

MARILYN LANFEAR

Since earning her M.F.A. in December 1978, Marilyn Lanfear has exhibited in the United States and in Central and South America. Coming from a strong formalist background, her work has emerged into a symbolist statement, always autobiographical. Her drawings, sculptures, and performances, while personally psychological in origin, are generalized into social commentary. Sometimes they comment on men and women, sometimes on social status, sometimes on the kind of image individuals try to project. Lanfear is a native Texan whose work has been exhibited in Texas at the Witte Museum, the McNay Art Institute, the San Antonio Art Institute, the Dallas Museum of Fine Art, and the Laguna Gloria Art Museum in Austin, as well as at the Museu de Monterrey, Museo de Arte Contemporanea da Universidade de São Paulo, and a number of alternative spaces, including the steps of the San Antonio Museum of Art.

ELLEN LANYON

Born in Chicago, Ellen Lanyon's formal art training includes a B.F.A. from the Art Institute of Chicago, an M.F.A. from the State University of Iowa, and technical studies at the Courtauld Institute, University of London, as a Fulbright Scholar. Since her professional career began in 1946, she has had fifty solo exhibitions and has participated in numerous group shows. Her work is in countless private and public collections, including the Art Institute of Chicago, the Library of Congress, the Metropolitan Museum, the McNay Art Institute in San Antonio, Texas, and the National Museum of American Art. She has been the recipient of Fulbright, Cassandra, Hereward Lester Cooke, and National Endowment for the Arts grants, and has been a fellow at Yaddo and the Ossabaw Island Project. Since 1952 she has taught, critiqued, and lectured at colleges and universities throughout the United States. She has been active on the board of the CAA and of OXBOW. Currently living in New York and teaching at the School of Visual Arts and Cooper Union, she also maintains a studio in Chicago.

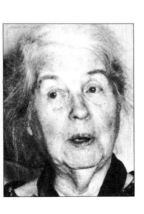

ALICE NEEL

Alice Neel was born in Merion Square, Pennsylvania. She is a B.F.A. graduate of the Philadelphia School of Design for Women (now Moore College of Art). Her work has been exhibited at the Museum of Modern Art and the Whitney Museum of American Art in New York; Dillard Institute, New Orleans; Graham Gallery in New York; and Moore College of Art. She has served as a lecturer at the University of Pennsylvania Graduate School and the Skowhegan School of Painting and Sculpture. A member of the American Academy of Arts and Letters, she received its Lett Award in 1969. She has also received the Longview Foundation Award and the National Academy of Design's Benjamin Altman Figure Prize. She was given a retrospective at the Whitney Museum of American Art in New York in 1974. Her work is in the permanent collections of: the Museum of Modern Art, Metropolitan Museum of Art, Whitney Museum of American Art, and Hirshhorn Museum and Sculpture Garden, among others.

BETTY PARSONS

Betty Parsons was born in New York. She began studying sculpture in New York, then moved to Paris where she studied with Bourdelle, Archipenko, and Zadkine. During her stay in Europe, she spent many summers in Brittany, where she studied with English painter Arthur Lindsay. She has had more than twenty one-woman exhibitions in Paris, London, Dublin, and throughout the United States. Her works have been included in exhibitions at the Museum of Modern Art, the Whitney Museum, and the American Academy of Arts and Letters, and are represented in the permanent collections of the Whitney Museum, the National Collection of Fine Arts, and the Rockefeller Institute. She died in July 1982.

FAITH RINGGOLD

A native New Yorker, Ringgold received her B.S. and M.F.A. degrees from the City College of New York. She has taught art to students from pre-kindergarten through college levels, and to teachers at the Bank Street College of Education Graduate School. Ringgold's paintings, sculptures, masks, and performances have been exhibited in museums and galleries in the United States, Europe, and Africa, including the Museum of Modern Art in New York City; her works are in many public and private collections, including the Chase Manhattan Bank Collection. Widely reviewed, Ringgold's art and life are documented in such publications as *Originals: American Women Artists* by Eleanor Munro; *From the Center* by Lucy Lippard, and *Who's Who Among Black Americans.* She has received many awards for her paintings and sculptures, including an individual grant from the National Endowment for the Arts, the Creative Artists Public Service Award from New York State, and the American Association of University Women. In April of 1984 the new Studio Museum in Harlem will hold a twenty-year retrospective of her work.

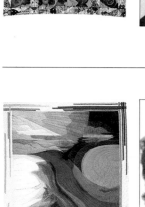

CHARLOTTE ROBINSON

Charlotte Robinson was born in San Antonio, Texas. She moved to New York City, where she attended New York University and the Art Students League, and then to Washington, D.C., where she studied with Eugene Weis at the Corcoran School of Art and was granted a scholarship in 1952. From 1960 to 1963 she lived and studied in Europe; exhibitions of her work were held in Madrid, Lisbon, and Paris. Her work has been shown extensively in the United States. Individual and group exhibitions include the Chrysler Museum, Norfolk, Virginia; the Mint Museum, Charlotte, North Carolina; San Jose (California) State University; and Rutgers University. Through the nonprofit Adhibit Committee she received National Endowment for the Arts grants in 1977, 1978, and 1981. Her work is in the permanent collections of the Museu Nacional De Arte Contemporanea, Lisbon, Portugal; the Museo Español De Arte Contemporaneo, Madrid, Spain; and the New School for Social Research, New York.

BETYE SAAR

Betye Saar was born in Los Angeles, California, and is a graduate of the University of California, Los Angeles. A well-known assemblage and collage artist, she has seen her works displayed at numerous solo and group exhibitions, including shows at the San Francisco Museum of Art, the Smithsonian Institution, Rutgers University, and the Whitney Museum. Her works are in the permanent collections of the University of Massachusetts, Amherst; Wellington Evest Collection, Boston; Golden State Mutual Life Insurance Collection; and the University of California at Berkeley. She has taught visual arts at the California State University, Hayward, Northridge, Long Beach, and has been the recipient of two purchase awards and an award from the National Endowment for the Arts. She was featured in the WNET-TV series on women artists in "Spiritcatcher: The Art of Betye Saar." She lives and works in Los Angeles and is currently teaching at the Otis Art Institute of Parsons School of Design.

MIRIAM SCHAPIRO

Miriam Schapiro was born in Toronto, Canada. She grew up in New York City and was educated at the University of Iowa, where she received her B.A., M.A., and M.F.A. She married painter Paul Brach; they lived in Columbia, Missouri, until 1952, when they returned to New York and became part of the group that met at the Cedar Bar and The Club. In 1954 they bought a home in Easthampton and have spent summers there ever since. Schapiro showed with the André Emmerich Gallery for sixteen years. In 1964 she and Brach worked at the Tamarind Lithography Workshop on a Ford Foundation grant. They returned to California to live in 1967, working first at University of California, San Diego, where Brach was chairman, and later at Cal Arts in Los Angeles, where he was dean. It was at Cal Arts that Schapiro and Judy Chicago created the art program "Womanhouse." In 1974 Schapiro returned to New York and formed the "Pattern and Decoration" group with Zakanitch, Kozloff, and others. She is currently associated with the Barbara Gladstone Gallery in New York, and her paintings are shown internationally. Public collections housing her works include the Hirshhorn Museum, the Museum of Modern Art, and the Whitney Museum.

ROSEMARY WRIGHT

Rosemary Wright was born in Richmond, Indiana. She was educated at Indiana University, Columbia University, and New York University, where she received her M.A. in 1970. Her career background includes work as a designer, ceramicist, sculptor, photographer, and performer. Solo exhibitions of her work have been shown in New York City, Washington, D.C., and Ohio State University. Galleries, museums, and colleges and universities throughout the United States as well as in Zurich and Milan have included her work in group exhibitions. She founded the D.C. Registry of Women Artists in 1972 and co-founded the Adhibit Committee, Inc., in 1973. She has been on the faculty of the Corcoran School of Art since 1973 and is presently co-chair of the junior year. She received a Ford Fellowship in 1981 to direct the Corcoran Summer Workshop in Maine. Most recently, her book *The Beech Tree Piece* has been seen in two national exhibitions of artists' books.

QUILTERS

AMY CHAMBERLIN

Amy Chamberlin was born in Canasota, New York. She received her B.F.A. in Art Education from Syracuse University. She has worked as a commercial artist for General Electric Corporation and for the National Wildlife Federation. From 1949 to 1953 she was the art supervisor and teacher in the public schools of Vinadilla and Groton, New York; from 1960 to 1967 she was art supervisor in the public schools of Paramus, New Jersey. From 1975 to the present, she has taught machine embroidery for adult education in the Montgomery and Prince George's Community Colleges in Maryland. Her awards include the 1979 First Prize in Embroidered Quilt from the National Quilter's Association.

BOB DOUGLAS

Barbara Zivi (Bob) Douglas grew up in Severna Park, Maryland. After college she lived in the Baltimore area for several years, then moved with her husband and two sons to a farm outside Berkeley Springs, West Virginia. She has been designing quilts and selling them to private collectors since 1974.

CHRIS WOLF EDMONDS

Chris Wolf Edmonds began quiltmaking in 1965. During the 1970s she became known for her translations of pictures into fabric for the quilt surface. She was commissioned by the *Saturday Evening Post, Good Housekeeping, Decorating and Craft Ideas, Needlecraft for Today,* and *Quilter's Newsletter Magazine* to translate or design original pieces. Her most recent "picture" quilt, *Prairie Pioneer,* was commissioned by the Lawrence Art Guild to hang in the new Lawrence, Kansas, City Hall, and was pictured on the cover of *Quilter's Newsletter Magazine,* March 1983. Her quilts have won awards in shows throughout the country, and she travels extensively across the United States and Canada lecturing and conducting quilt design workshops. She works out of a studio in her home near Lawrence, Kansas, where she lives with her husband and two children.

THERESA LANFEAR HELMS

Theresa Lanfear Helms was born in Fort Smith, Arkansas, on April 29, 1953. She attended Austin College and the University of Dallas, receiving a B.A. in 1979, and an M.A. and an M.F.A. in 1980. Helms is a painter who works with metal, dyes, and paper. She has exhibited in Dallas, Austin, Fort Worth, San Antonio, and various other cities throughout the South. She is currently working as a designer of children's clothing for Malley & Co. in Dallas.

MARIE GRIFFIN INGALLS

Marie Griffin Ingalls was born near Jamesville, in Martin County, North Carolina. Interested in art as early as she can remember, she pursued her art studies with private instructors, including the late Sadie Ingalls Vaden of Potomac, Maryland, and Daniel B. Mistrik of the Mistrik School of Art in Bethesda, Maryland. She recently toured Europe, visiting art galleries, to further her knowledge and understanding of art. In addition to her artistry with quilts, Ingalls's many needlecraft skills include couturier clothing, crewel embroidery, and unique cloth doll creations with hand-painted faces. Her greatest love, however, is painting, using oils as a medium, and she has won several blue ribbons for her canvases. One of her recently completed larger projects is the authentic history of the Maryland Gold Mine, depicted in a series of oil paintings that are now a part of the Maryland Gold Mine Museum.

ANGELA JACOBI

Her interest in needlework started at a very young age and was part of the training girls of her heritage [Greek] had at home. She has used this talent in many ways all her life. She has made costumes for plays at school and church. In New York City, she attended the evening classes at the Needle Trade High School and made costumes for a small ballet company. Many of her quilt designs came from the graphic design problems her brother, Nicholas Chaparos, created while at Hochschule für Gestaltung in Ulm, Germany. She has studied sculpture at Arizona State University, and at the School of Art at the Art Institute of Chicago, and studied Indian pottery with Maria Martinez. She ran, with two other artists, a small art center in Chicago and is currently with the University of Wisconsin, Milwaukee, as a Museum Specialist.

JUDY MATHIESON

Judy Mathieson is a nationally recognized quiltmaker who has been teaching since 1977. She became interested in quiltmaking while completing her B.S. in Home Economics—Textiles and Clothing at California State University, Northridge. She teaches regularly at local Los Angeles fabric shops, lectures and conducts workshops throughout the United States, and has designed and marketed several quilt and garment patterns. She served as a consultant and needleworker for eight months on Judy Chicago's *Dinner Party* project in 1978. Selected for the juried show "Quilt National" in Athens, Ohio, in 1979 and 1981, her quilts are shown on their poster and in the book *The New American Quilt*. Several of her quilts and garments were shown on the public television series *Quilting* in 1981. Her work is frequently featured in *Quilter's Newsletter Magazine*.

SHARON MCKAIN

Sharon McKain has been teaching quilting since 1970 and is a frequent lecturer for community groups. She has exhibited her work in California, Mexico, Rhode Island, and Connecticut. Her awards include First Prize in the Annual Juried Show, Mystic Art Association, Connecticut, 1974 and 1979, and an honorable mention in the National Quilt Contest in Santa Rosa, California. In 1974 she was awarded a grant from the Connecticut Commission on the Arts. Author of *The Great Noank Quilt Factory*, she lives and works in Providence, Rhode Island.

EDITH C. MITCHELL

Having raised a family, she launched a new career as a professional quilter in 1973, exhibiting work at craft fairs in Vermont and upstate New York. The following year she became owner/manager of Blue Mountain Designs, a craft shop/gallery in Blue Mountain Lake, New York, in the heart of the Adirondack Mountains. The new business allowed time for quilting, and a rapid succession of exhibits of work at galleries, fairs, and art centers followed—in the Adirondacks, elsewhere in New York State, in Baltimore, Philadelphia, and Columbus. During this time she also began to teach, first at the Adirondack Lakes Center for the Arts, then one-month stints as artisan-in-residence in Glens Falls and Malone, New York, and a tour of duty with American Waterways Floating Center for the Arts, traveling through seven southern states. For the past few years she has taught quilting at North Country Community College. For a complete change of pace from quilting, teaching, and running a business, she now escapes during the winters to a small ski-touring lodge near Saranac Lake, where she creates meals for very hungry and highly appreciative skiers—and in the process has become an avid cross-country skier.

THE MITCHELL FAMILY

The Mitchell Family Quilt celebrates four generations. Fred (1890–1975) and Lulu Seaney (1892–1965) were the parents, grandparents, and great-grandparents of the women who created the quilt. The image of Fred and Lulu, the featured center square, is from a photo taken on their fiftieth wedding anniversary in 1964. From 1850, when Fred's grandparents came to Indiana from Ireland, the family was mostly farmers. Now there are teachers, artists, dressmakers, engineers, government workers, factory laborers, real estate agents, a priest, and a pre-med student. Along with their Irish heritage, the Catholic faith was bequeathed to the family by their ancestors. They came from large families, eight to fifteen children, and most enjoyed long lives. Fred's mother died at age eighty-nine. Although all the present members were born and raised in Indiana, and most remain in the Richmond and Indianapolis areas, one granddaughter lives in Washington, D.C. and a great-granddaughter lives in San Francisco, California.

PAT NEWKIRK

Born in Morehead, Kentucky, Pat Newkirk is a quiltmaker, writer, teacher, and lecturer. In addition to creating her own quilts, Newkirk has devoted much of her energy to teaching others quiltmaking in home economics departments, recreation programs, and classes for independent quilting teachers. While working full time, she is also currently completing work for a B.S. at the University of Maryland and has been accepted for graduate studies. Newkirk does freelance writing about quiltmaking for *The Clarion* (The Museum of American Folk Art), *Patchwork Platter* (The National Quilt Association), and assorted other publications. She was editor for *Polly Prindle's Book of American Patchwork Quilts*, and is currently working on a textbook of quiltmaking to be used by both teachers and students.

BONNIE PERSINGER

Bonnie Persinger grew up in North Carolina, Florida, and Louisiana. She began making quilts after migrating to Maryland in 1972. Her quilts have won many national awards and Persinger (then Boudra) was included in many national juried shows including "Young Americans: Fiber/Wood/Plastic/Leather," sponsored by the American Crafts Council. A frequent lecturer and teacher at quilt conferences and craft workshops, she emphasizes innovative designs and new techniques. In recent years her interest in quiltmaking has had to compete with the demands of her position as Design and Drafting Manager for a rapidly growing computer manufacturer. She currently lives in Annapolis, Maryland.

WILLI POSEY

Born March 22, 1907, in Palatka, Florida, Willi Posey was educated at The Central Academy, Palatka, Florida; Wadleigh High School, New York City; and the Fashion Institute of Technology, New York City. A dressmaker and fashion designer, she participated in exhibitions at the New York Hilton, The Abyssinian Fashion Show, and the NAACP Show of Shows. She was a member of the National Association of Fashion and Accessory Designers, the National Council of Negro Women, and The Overseas Club Abyssinian Baptist Church. She died in October 1981.

MARILYN PRICE

Marilyn Price's youth was spent in southern Missouri. She learned needle skills from her seamstress mother at a very early age. As an art major at Pittsburg State University in Kansas she studied printmaking, concentrating on silk-screen, which has been her preferred medium throughout her career. She has done graduate study at the Kansas City Art Institute, University of Tennessee, Arrowmont, and the Instituto Allende, San Miguel de Allende, Guanajuato, Mexico. While at Arrowmont in the mid-1970s Price transferred her screenprinting from paper to fabric. She uses a combination of screenprinted and embellished fabric to create large commissioned wallhangings for architectural spaces. She has exhibited in juried and solo shows extensively; her work is shown in galleries in New York, Indiana, and Arizona, and is included in numerous private collections.

NANCY VOGEL

Nancy Vogel was born in Albuquerque, New Mexico. She attended Texas Tech University in Lubbock, Texas, majoring in clothing and textiles. After relocating to Connecticut in 1970, Vogel became a student of and then apprentice to quilt artist Sharon McKain. She moved to Florida in 1978 and taught quiltmaking at the Grove House in Coconut Grove. Returning to the Southwest in 1980, Nancy now resides and works in El Paso, Texas. She does one-of-a-kind commissions, and gives workshops and teaches quilting at the El Paso Community College.

WENDA F. VON WEISE

Wenda von Weise received her B.F.A. in 1975 in textile design with a minor in photography from the Cleveland Institute of Art, Cleveland, Ohio, where she received the Nancy E. Dunn Memorial Traveling Scholarship. In December 1978 von Weise completed her M.F.A. degree in fibers at Cranbrook Academy of Art, Bloomfield Hills, Michigan. She is currently assistant professor of Surface Design at the Cleveland Institute of Art. Von Weise specializes in printing photographic images on fabric for quilts and quilted wall pieces. She received an Individual Artist Fellowship Grant from the Ohio Arts Council in 1980. She was included in the 1980 "Art for Use," commissioned by the National Fine Arts Committee of the XIII Olympic Games at the American Craft Museum in New York City and earlier exhibited at the same museum in "The New American Quilt" exhibition. Recent and scheduled exhibitions include the Cleveland Museum of Art, "the Cleveland Museum of Art: 100 Years," January 1984; "Artspace," Sign of the Swan Gallery, Philadelphia (1982); St. Mary's Art Gallery, Halifax, Nova Scotia (1982); "Ohio Quilts 1880–1980," the Canton Art Institute, Canton, Ohio (1982); the Ohio State Fair Fine Arts Exhibition (1981); "Quilt National," Athens, Ohio (1981); and "Contemporary Quilts," the University of Wisconsin's statewide traveling exhibition (1981).

INDEX

CREDITS

FOR THE EXHIBITION

Grants/Foundations
National Endowment for the Arts
Mary Duke Biddle Foundation
Adhibit Committee, Inc.
WBGU T.V., Bowling Green, Ohio
North Carolina Museum of Art
Corporate Donations
Philip Morris Inc.
**Patron for Opening Activities at the Marion Koogler
   McNay Art Institute, San Antonio, Texas**
Arthur Young & Company
Contributing Friend
Marubeni of America

FOR THE BOOK

Photography and Illustrations
Michelle Wise Alyea: page 96
Terry Arthur: pages 10, 13 (bottom), 57
Courtesy Betty Parsons Gallery: page 68
Paul Boudra, Jr.: page 63
Joel Breger: pages 8-9, 48-49, 53, 55, 58, 61, 64, 68, 72, 75-76,
   78, 84, 87, 90, 94, 100, 103, 109, 111, 114-115
Katherine Clark: pages 60, 105
Courtesy DAR Museum: pages 17, 18, 20-21, 22-23
D. James Dee: page 91
Mary Beth Edelson: pages 73-74
Cynthia Farah: page 110
Courtesy Ronald Feldman Fine Arts, New York: pages 34
   (Eeva-Inkeri), 42
Alan Finkelman: page 109
Julian Goff: page 13 (top)
Maynard Hicks: page 62
John Kluesener: pages 67, 69
Larry McIntire: pages 112-113
Midtown Galleries, New York: page 101
Jerry Nataro: pages 14, 93, 97, 117
Kevin Noble: pages 28-29, 30
Kate Roberts: page 102
Charlotte Robinson: pages 12, 77, 89 (right),
Daphne Shuttleworth: all photos and line drawings for
   "Design and Construction"
Courtesy Smithsonian Institution: pages 19, 24, 27
Mary Swift: pages 15 (bottom left), 81
Joyce Tenneson: page 116
Lyndia Terr: page 15 (top left and right, bottom right)
Courtesy Through the Flower, Inc., Benicia, California: page 35
Sarah Tuft: page 80
*Collection of the Whitney Museum of American Art, Gift of the
   Dietrich Brothers Americana Corporation*: page 37

About The Authors

CHARLOTTE ROBINSON is an artist, teacher, and writer. Through the nonprofit Adhibit Committee she received National Endowment for the Arts grants in 1977, 1978, and 1981. Her work has been shown internationally, and is in the permanent collections of the Museo Español de Arte Contemporaneo, Madrid, Spain; Museu Nacional de Arte Contemporanea, Lisbon, Portugal; and New School for Social Research, New York City. She lives in Falls Church, Virginia.

JEAN TAYLOR FEDERICO is the Director of the Daughters of the American Revolution (DAR) Museum in Washington, D.C. She is a frequent lecturer on American decorative arts and needlework. She has written for the magazine *Antiques* and *The Clarion, America's Folk Magazine*.

MIRIAM SCHAPIRO is an internationally known artist, whose work is included in the public collections at the Hirshhorn Museum and Sculpture Garden, Museum of Modern Art, and Whitney Museum of American Art. With Judy Chicago she created the art program "Womanhouse." In 1974 Schapiro helped organize the "Pattern and Decoration" group in New York City.

LUCY R. LIPPARD is a writer and critic of contemporary art. She is a contributing editor for *Art in America*, where her articles appear regularly. Her most recent book is *Overlay: Contemporary Art and the Art of Prehistory*.

ELEANOR MUNRO is a well-known writer on the arts. Her latest book is *Originals: American Women Artists*. She has published essays, reviews, and journalistic articles in many national magazines and those specializing in the arts and letters.

BONNIE (BOUDRA) PERSINGER, award-winning quilter from Maryland, has had her quilts exhibited nationally. She has lectured and conducted workshops throughout the United States on the art of quilting.

DAPHNE SHUTTLEWORTH is art director of the Office of Folk Life Programs at the Smithsonian Institution in Washington, D.C.